Greek Island Cooking

Or

The Short and Happy
Tale of Pippo Alampo

Sara Alexi is the author of the Greek Village Series
and the Greek Island Series

She divides her time between England and a small
village in Greece.

http://facebook.com/authorsaraalexi

Sara Alexi
GREEK ISLAND COOKING
Or
The Short and Happy
Tale of Pippo Alampo

ISBN: 9781521755860

oneiro

Published by Oneiro Press 2017

Copyright © Sara Alexi 2017

This book is a work of fiction. Names, characters, businesses, organisations, places and events are either the product of the author's imagination or are used fictitiously. Any resemblance to actual persons, living or dead, events or locales is entirely coincidental

Also by Sara Alexi

The Illegal Gardener
Black Butterflies
The Explosive Nature of Friendship
The Gypsy's Dream
The Art of Becoming Homeless
In the Shade of the Monkey Puzzle Tree
A Handful of Pebbles
The Unquiet Mind
Watching the Wind Blow
The Reluctant Baker
The English Lesson
The Priest's Well
A Song Amongst the Orange Trees
The Stolen Book
The Rush Cutter's Legacy
Saving Septic Cyril
The Piano Raft
The Greek Village Colouring Book
The Housekeeper
An Island Too Small

Introduction

I make no secret of the fact that I'm not the world's best cook!

Luckily for me most traditional Greek dishes are easy to make and forgiving of my mistakes…

Quantities are not critical, and most of the recipes presented here can be made in many different ways, with any number of local variations. If you don't have a particular ingredient to hand, don't be afraid to experiment – who knows, you may come up with something new and delicious! (If you do, be sure to write and let me know!)

I've included a selection of my favourites – simple, tasty and wholesome treats that never fail to please.

And of course, I couldn't resist writing a story too!

Enjoy!

Sara Alexi

Chapter 1

'What a woman,' Mitsos muses to himself as he takes the *briki* off the heat and pours coffee into a tiny mug.

He turns off the gas, swills the *briki* under the tap and replaces it on its hook by the stove, and steps out into the unpaved yard at the back of the cottage. Around the edges, old olive oil tins have been used as planters, for geraniums mainly, with the occasional weed balancing a yellow flower on a spidery stem. He wanders to the side of the cottage, from where there is a view of the whole village and the plain beyond that stretches out towards the hills in the far distance, a patchwork of fields and orange orchards. Two more strides and he is at the front of his house, a narrow patio with a plastic chair. It is enough.

'What a woman,' he says to himself again, sipping the sweet liquid. Three years has not been long enough to come to terms with his new status—not after sixty years or so as a single man—and to such a fine woman as Stella!

Behind him, beyond the house, up past the chicken coop, the top of the hill is crested with pine trees which rustle and whisper in the slight breeze. The little stone house where he has lived all his life is on the outskirts of the village, halfway up the little hill that rises out of the flat plain between the village and Saros. This hill blocks the view in the direction of the town but provides an elevated position from which Mitsos can see more or less everything that goes on in the village.

The house was built by Mitsos's *propappous*—his father's grandfather—in a time when the Turks still occupied Greece and there were no more than a handful of houses dotted about the plain. Now he has plenty of neighbours, but not enough to find him a wife until so recently.

'Three years!' he marvels. 'And yet now I could not imagine life without her.' Another sip of coffee and a smack of the lips. In the village square below, he can make out Theo with a tray in one hand, collecting cups and glasses from the tables spread on the square across from the kafenio. Just to the side of the tables, Vasso will be in her kiosk, where the day's newspapers are pegged around the edge of the roof like washing. When Mitsos was a boy, it was just a small wooden box, selling cigarettes and sweets, but in recent years it has expanded, and now there are two drink cabinets and a chest freezer for ice creams. Marina's corner shop, across the road from the kiosk, is open too, and two women stand in the doorway chatting. The pharmacy is dark; it so seldom seems to be open these days.

Mitsos's scrutiny of the village is distracted by a rustling in the dried grass that surrounds the rough stone patio at the front of the house. As he searches for the cause, a gnarled prehistoric head lumbers into view.

'There you are,' Mitsos says gently. He has no fresh lettuce today, but there is a piece, somewhat wilted from the day before, on the table by his cup. He leans down and places it directly in front of the tortoise's nose, and the ancient reptile examines it briefly, then chews with deliberation.

'Three years, *helona*,' he tells the tortoise. 'Next week is our anniversary. We must do something really special to mark it.' The tortoise continues to munch, unimpressed by Mitsos's achievement. 'This week she is away,' he continues, undeterred by the animal's indifference, 'at a trade fair in Athens. So what do you say we think of something to surprise her? A gift? A party? I wonder what she would like…'

But the tortoise, which has finished munching on the lettuce leaf, simply turns and stamps away and is soon hidden again by the dried grass. Mitsos's coffee is finished too, and he glances at his watch, noting that he should already be down in the village, opening up the eatery.

On bad days he leans heavily on his crook, but on good days, like today, he hardly needs it at all and only carries it out of habit. But his gait, as he makes his way down the dusty lane and into the village square, is still bent and his progress is slow, if steady. As he turns the key in the lock, Mitsos notes that he left the lights on again, and not just the one inside. Outside, a string of tiny lights is wound round and round the tree on the pavement, lighting up the chairs and tables there. Stella insists this attracts people, although he cannot see it himself. He must remember to turn them off tonight. A few dirty glasses and a plate are stacked on top of the counter where he left them last night, and behind this, the embers in the grill are still glowing. Mitsos has learned to adapt over the years, but some jobs are difficult with only one arm. The charcoal bag is heavy and awkward. He lifts it, jams it against the grill with his knee, reaches for the scissors to cut off the corner, then lifts further until it tips and spills its contents into the grill.

'Enough,' he says to himself and sets the bag down again, puffing slightly with the exertion. In the fridge, the chickens are cleaned and ready to go on the grill, and Stella made enough lemon sauce to last three weeks, let alone just the one that she will be away! She has also left a huge bag of ready-cut chips, so that he will not have to struggle with peeling and slicing potatoes while she is away. There are some courgettes that need using up though. He can fry those this morning in a little olive oil, and offer them as hors d'ouvres to whoever comes in first.

'Stella,' he sighs, 'what can I give you? What would you like? You who are always taking care of me, and of most of the farmers in the village when they need feeding in here, to say nothing of all the guests at our little hotel!' He refers to the place they recently acquired down by the beach. 'What would you really like?' He pours lighter fuel over the charcoal, which catches immediately from the glowing embers. 'A necklace? A ring? A bangle? A dress?'

'Who are you talking to then?' Cosmo the postman calls in from out on the pavement. He kicks the stand down on his bike but does not turn off the engine.

'To myself, Cosmo! I was just enquiring of myself what Stella would like for our third wedding anniversary.'

'Three years already! And yet I cannot imagine you two ever apart. You have a postcard here from Athens.'

'It will be from Stella.'

'Maybe it says what gift she would like?' Cosmo laughs.

'More likely it will be to remind me to order more charcoal.' Mitsos wipes his hands on a tea towel and takes the card, examines the oversaturated picture of the Acropolis and then turns it over, squints at the writing, and laughs. 'Yup, she says "Miss you lots. It is very interesting. Don't forget to order more charcoal."' Mitsos chuckles and Cosmo laughs out loud.

'Well, you'd best not forget then.' Cosmo swings his leg over the bike and is just about to drive away when his attention is caught by the sight of a young man standing in the square looking rather lost.

Mitsos follows his stare and now he too looks at the youth, a small frown creasing his forehead. The boy, who cannot be out of his teens, could be Greek, judging by his features and his curly dark hair, but his skin is pale, as if he has not spent time out of doors, and his jeans and t-shirt are un-ironed, suggesting there is no one to look after him. The youth sees them looking and he turns towards the eatery, stepping across the square with a measured, easy tread.

Fried Courgettes / Zucchini

This is a super simple, tasty snack or accompaniment.

Ingredients:
2 lbs (1 kg) Courgette / Zucchini
Pepper, Salt
Flour
Olive oil for frying

Directions

Wash the courgettes / zucchini and cut into 1/4-inch slices.

In a large shallow dish mix salt and pepper into flour. Dip each courgette / zucchini slice into the seasoned flour and shake off any excess.

Fry a few courgette / zucchini slices at a time in olive oil until golden brown.

Serve with skordalia (see chapter 6) or tzatziki dipping sauces.

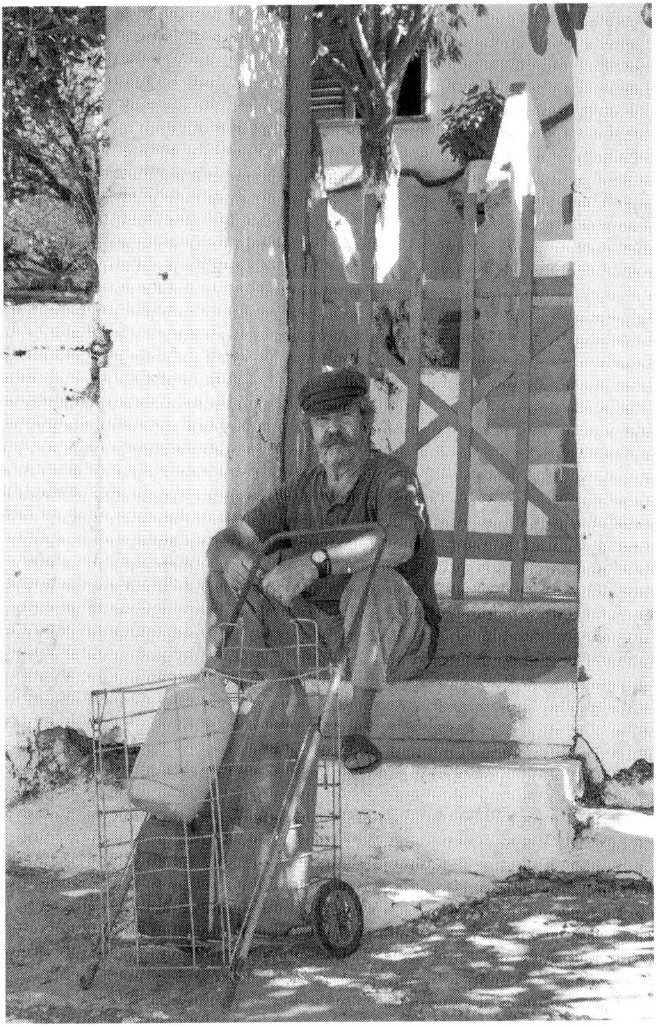

Tzatziki

One of the easiest and tastiest of the Greek dips, tzatziki combines creamy yoghurt, cool cucumber and a garlic punch... Everyone's favourite!

It's important to use good Greek yoghurt if you can get it. Use full fat – tzatziki should be rich and creamy!

Ingredients

150g (5oz) Greek yoghurt.

1/2 cucumber.

2 - 4 crushed garlic cloves.

1 tbsp olive oil.

1 tsp lemon juice (or white wine vinegar)

1 tsp chopped or dried mint (or dill)

1/2 tsp salt.

Pepper to taste.

Directions

Grate the cucumber with a cheese grater, then squeeze out as much of the liquid as you can. One way to do this is to wrap the grated cucumber in a clean cloth and squeeze over the sink.

Then simply stir all the ingredients into the yoghurt and enjoy!

Chapter 2

'*Yeia sou,*' Mitsos greets the young stranger as he approaches the door.

'Ciao.' The youth tosses his head back to shake the curls out of his face.

'The chicken isn't even on the grill yet. Chips will take more than a few minutes, but a frappe is fairly instant if you want something to wet your lips?' Mitsos pulls out a chair from under one of the tables on the pavement.

'Yes, a coffee. Good.' The boy's Greek is accented, and he sounds as though he wants to sing the words.

Inside, Mitsos whisks up coffee with sugar and a little water. 'Milk, sugar?' he calls and an answer is given. He tops the beverage with chilled milk and adds a couple of ice cubes.

The tall glasses sparkle back out in the sunshine.

'Here you go. I made myself one too. I have to wait for the grill to heat before I can do anything else today.' Mitsos pulls out the chair opposite. They sit in silence for a while, sucking on their straws and enjoying the morning's warmth.

'Where are you from?' Mitsos asks after a pause.

'Italy.' The young man lilts the word.

'*Una fatsa una ratsa*. Same face same race, as they say.' Mitsos knocks his glass against his companion's. The ice rattles.

'Exactly,' the stranger replies.

He was like that once, Mitsos recalls, all smooth skin over taut muscles and now his one arm is thin, the skin sagging. The boy is looking, but trying not to be obvious, at his other arm, his empty sleeve.

'Oh, I lost that a long time ago. Don't feel uncomfortable on my behalf,' Mitsos says to put the boy at his ease. 'Rather foolishly playing with dynamite.'

'When you were young?' He seems unimpressed.

'When I was old enough to know better.'

They sit and sip their drinks in silence. The morning air is still fresh, the full heat of the day yet to come.

'Are you hungry?' Mitsos asks and his stomach grumbles so loudly as he says this that they both smile at the timing. 'I fancy *ladovreckto*, and you would be welcome to share. As my guest.' He adds this qualifier when he catches just the trace of a frown pass across the youth's forehead.

'You'll never get rich that way.' The young man feels in his front pocket. Coins jingle.

'There are different kinds of riches. So I take that as a yes? You will join me?'

'What is *ladovreckto*?'

'You can understand a lot of Greek by breaking the words up, *lado*, from *lathi*, is…'

'Oil.'

'Right! And *vreckto* is...'

'To get wet.'

'There you go then. Wetted with oil.'

'Oil on bread then?' Another frown tickles at his eyebrow.

'Ah, how simply put! But what you do not know is that the bread made in this village has just a little honey added, as well as the olive oil. And the oil itself… How can I express it! Come. I will show you and you can try it and then decide.'

The coffees are abandoned, leaving the sun to melt the ice cubes. Inside, the grill is now warm and Mitsos takes an end of bread.

'This is yesterday's bread, but for *ladovreckto*, it is perfect.' Mitsos puts four slices on the grill. 'Now we take a little dried oregano and I put it in a bowl and crush it with a spoon. When I had two arms, I would put the herb in one hand and use the thumb of the other, with a little twist, and that would crush it up. Here, smell.'

'That's good,' the boy agrees. 'Now I do feel hungry.'

Mitsos turns the bread so that the first side, now toasted, is uppermost, striped from the bars of the grill.

'Now, you can wait until both sides are toasted, but having a grill gives me the advantage.' Mitsos picks up a bottle of thick green oil which he pours into a second dish and, with a pastry brush, he paints the hot toast where it sits on the heat. 'This is the best oil, the first cold pressing from my olives up the hill there.' He nods towards the door. 'So thick, so tasty, I don't know how people can eat that thin yellow stuff they sell in the supermarkets!'

'Because they have no choice?' the youth offers.

'Alas, that could be true. You see how the oil is soaking in but leaving the outside toasty? That's what you want. Now off the grill and sprinkle well with the oregano. A pinch of salt, and there you go.' He offers a plate with two slices to his new friend. 'Come,' he says when he has sprinkled his own slices. 'Let us sit in the sunshine and enjoy our simple breakfast.'

The stranger leads and Mitsos adds to his plate some tomatoes he picked yesterday from the vines up at the house.

'Here, little red sweets to go with your *ladovreckto*.'
They eat in silence.

Mitsos mops the last crumbs up with his wetted thumb. 'So, I am Mitsos.'

'Pippo. Short for Giuseppe, not Fillipo.' Pippo is a slow eater and still has half a slice on his plate. 'This is really good, by the way, for something so simple.'

'Do you like cooking?'

'Never learnt. My mama is all posh ready meals and take-aways. But whenever we are in a restaurant, I try to sit near the kitchens. I love those new places where everything is open plan and you can see the chefs at work.'

'So where is your mama?'

'At home in Forte de Marmi, Italy.'

'Are you here alone?'

'I am taking a year out and I thought I would find my family. My surname is Alampo, which is from this region, if I am not mistaken. Although we have been in Italy for four generations now, and anyone who would have known where the name comes from is dead. All I know is that my family came from somewhere around here.'

Mitsos scratches at the prickly hairs on his neck. 'Well, there's the name Alamanos round here and Galampos in the next village… do you have any more information?'

'No.'

'Okay, change of subject. What shall I get my wife for our third anniversary?'

'Your thirtieth anniversary?'

'No, our third.'

'You were in no hurry, were you?' Pippo takes the last corner of his *ladovreckto* and chews thoughtfully. 'Well, give her this for breakfast for sure. It's delicious for something so simple.'

'She's had had it a million times,' says Mitsos. 'She set this place up, this eatery. It had only four tables inside when she took it on, and now we have four outside as well. Then just as things were going smoothly, she took on a small hotel down that way by the sea.' Mitsos waves his arm. 'She has a team of two chefs there, but even so, she spends most of her days cooking, preparing food, and serving.'

'So there you have your answer.' Pippo talks as slowly as he eats, as if there is no hurry at all in life. His curly dark hair has fallen over his eyes again and he tosses his head to flick it out of the way. 'Give her a day when she does no cooking or serving at all, but other people cook and serve for her.'

Mitsos smiles at the idea but as he thinks over it, he can imagine Stella laughing at the novelty. He could cook for her, or perhaps, yes, he can ask her friends in the village to contribute too.

'You know, Pippo, I think that is genius. Seriously genius. Stella would just love that! She is never happier than when she is with a group of her friends at a table, even though she has the appetite of a bird. She will sit for hours, laughing and enjoying the banter.' And still nodding, and chuckling to himself, Mitsos takes the plates inside and tests the grill to see if it is hot. He should really put on more charcoal but that means lifting and pouring the bag over the hot grill, and it also means he will need to order more charcoal sooner and that is never easy, hauling the bags and stacking them with only one arm. Maybe when he was a bit younger, but now it does seem like hard work. He pokes at the grill with the tongs. He should definitely add more charcoal or it is not going to be enough to cook the chicken through, and then he will have to take them off, pour the charcoal, clean the grill, and replace the chicken. There is no shortcut.

He drags the charcoal bag from the corner where the aprons hang and heaves it up, bracing it with his knee. The only thing is that now the grill is hot, he must do this against the serving counter or the thick paper of the charcoal bag will singe and later tear. Shifting it up against the counter, the trick is to put it over his knee whilst he balances on one leg, brace the sealed end of the bag on the serving counter, and lower his knee so the charcoal pours down. He knows how ridiculous he looks doing this, and wishes he had not cut corners when he laid the fire in the first place.

'That looks awkward. Here, let me give you a hand.' Pippo has come in, and Mitsos can feel his cheeks flush. He had hoped to finish the manoeuvre without the boy noticing. Pippo takes the bag with the greatest of ease, pours a quantity of charcoal into the grill, folds the top over, and puts it back on the floor.

'Two hands,' Mitsos shrugs, and smiles thinly. 'Very useful.'

Pippo puts his hands in his front pockets and stands in the doorway, his face towards the sun, his eyes closed.

'If you were me, how would you find your relatives?'

'Never had the problem, I'm afraid. My family have always lived here. I have an older brother in Corinth and a younger one in Saros. I can't imagine what you can actually do.' Mitsos rubs at the grill bars with the wire brush, cleaning them up, ready for the chickens.

'That's what I am thinking. What am I actually going to do?'

'I suppose you need to meet people, ask them questions.'

'I can hardly knock door to door.' Pippo seems to find this funny and his frame shakes as he chuckles quietly to himself.

'Well, you could do worse than hang about here. Most people come in here sooner or later.'

Pippo turns his head. 'I would get bored just hanging about.'

'Yes, I suppose. But you know,' Mitsos muses, 'my wife is gone for the week, and I, as you have just seen, am struggling with some of the jobs on my own. What if I offer you a bit of a job here? It would be a great way to casually meet people, ask all the questions you like. Also I think I would enjoy your company. What do you think?'

There is no grin of excitement, no sudden burst of energy, but Pippo turns and faces Mitsos, looking him square in the eyes.

'Alright,' he says, and they shake hands.

Ladovreckto

Grilled bread or λαδοβρεχτό is the simplest way to enjoy a loaf of good bread.

The bread needs to be not too crumbly nor too mushy. You need good, thick slices to soak up the simple flavours.

Whilst the bread is grilling crush some dried oregano. Turn the bread around as it grills so it is evenly golden brown. It wants to toast quickly so as to make the outside crisp but keep the inside soft.

Then straight from the heat, brush each piece generously with extra virgin Greek olive oil, the oil that is almost green in colour.

It makes a big difference if you do this immediately after taking the bread from the grill as the outside remains crisply toasted but the flavour of the olive oil soaks inside.

Sprinkle with coarse sea salt and the oregano. It is unbelievably tasty and could not be any easier.

It is also good with crushed basil or roasted garlic, and if there are tomatoes on the vine pick them, dice finely and add as a topping.

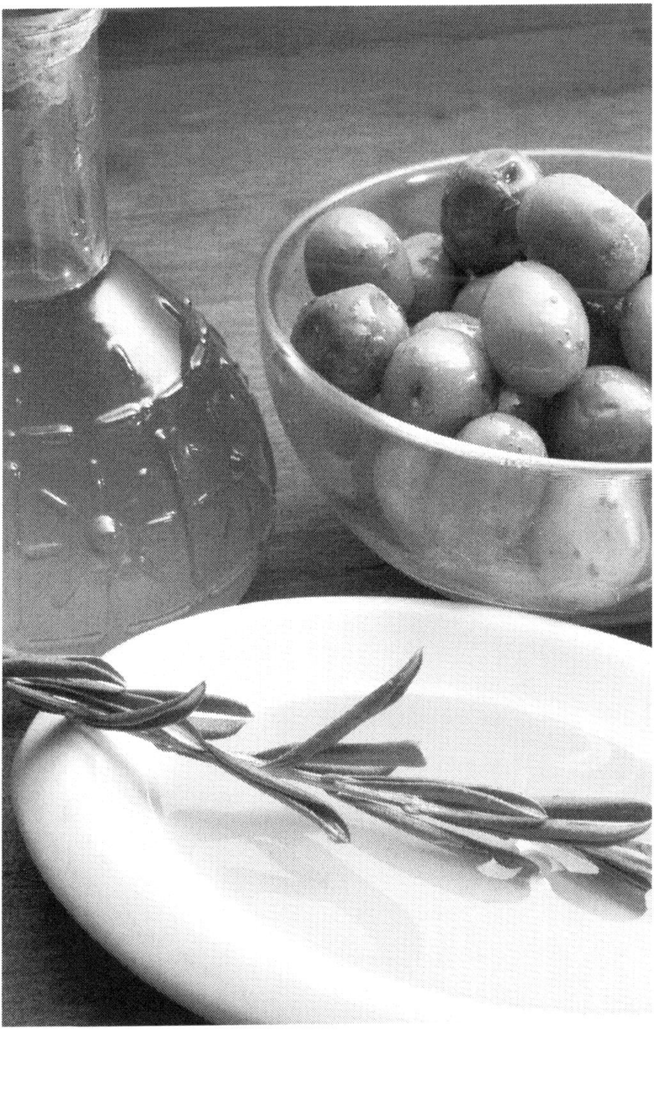

Chapter 3

'So that's the plan then.' The eatery is not busy yet. The chickens are on the grill, some chips have been made and served to an early bird, but until lunchtime, Mitsos knows that most of the day will be spent waiting. There will be a sudden rush after midday, and a few farmers will hang on for a beer or two as the day stretches into the late afternoon, and then another lull. A second rush will come at dinnertime when farmers who are single, or widowed, wander down to the square in the evening, and there will be some take-aways too: chicken, chips and salad, and a generous helping of Stella's lemon sauce. But for now he can sit and watch the comings and goings in the village square.

'It sounds like a good plan,' Pippo agrees.

'Look, here comes Vasso. Vasso runs the kiosk in the square, and Stella has known her since forever. Let's see if she approves of our plan.'

Introductions are made and Mitsos launches into the details. 'You know it is our anniversary next week,' he explains. 'Three years since we got married and, well, I thought we would put a long table at the back of the house and invite everyone. But the plan is for Stella to do none of the cooking, and instead have everyone serving on her and for her to sit like a queen.'

'Ha, Stella sit and do nothing! That will be a first.' Vasso starts to laugh heartily at her own joke.

'Exactly, but I thought if we each made her a dish, she would have to accept that she could not get involved with the cooking. And, having talked it over with my friend Pippo here, we decided that we would grill the chickens here at the eatery and ask each of the guests to bring one vegetable dish. What do you think?'

'Or a sweet dish! I make a great baklava.' Vasso seems enthusiastic.

'Yes, of course. I forgot about sweets. Although she does not tend to eat sweet food.'

'But I do, and so do Marina and Maria, and Juliet and…'

'Yes, you are right!' Mitsos laughs. 'So, maybe one sweet and one vegetable dish each?'

'Make the sweet recipe optional,' Pippo suggests, and all three nod seriously.

'So, do you want me to make this dish or tell you how to make it, or what? Oh, and can I have a small portion of chips for now? I'm starving.' She turns to check on the kiosk, where a man is standing waiting to be served. 'Hang on,' she says and then adds in English, 'I'll be back,' which she seems to find extremely funny, and she chuckles to herself all the way across to the kiosk. Mitsos and Pippo watch Vasso dip her beautifully coiffured head into the low rear doorway at the back of the hut.

'She must use a lot of hair lacquer,' Pippo says.

'A good woman,' Mitsos replies.

They watch her serve her customer, and then follow his progress across the road and into the kafenio. Vasso reappears out of the back of her hut, goes across the road into the corner shop, and comes out a few minutes later with a heavy pan and a bulging plastic bag. They watch as she approaches and Pippo jumps up with more haste than Mitsos would have given him credit for, relieving her of her burdens.

'Right.' Vasso is out of breath and a little red in the face. 'So this is a very easy recipe, but as tasty as they come. It is so simple a child can do it, but so filling. When I was a girl, we would often have this as a main course—nothing else, just this. But then in those days, no one ate as much meat as they do now. Although it goes well with all meat, really.'

She gives no pause for reply.

'Now, in the old days I would have you two boys sitting shelling peas all morning, nice little fresh, sweet, plump ones.' She giggles again. 'Peas, not boys,' she adds.

She cannot be more than eight or ten years younger than Mitsos; older than his wife for sure, but she still has this childlike propensity to laugh, mostly at her own jokes.

'But as I am just showing you, I have brought frozen peas.' She pulls out a stiff bag of frozen peas and smacks it against the table edge, loosening the contents.

Pippo looks at Mitsos, who raises his eyebrows in return. It never occurred to him that Vasso would be demonstrating her recipe immediately. Mitsos takes another look around the square but no one is about, so he shrugs and they follow Vasso inside to see her produce her dish.

'When I make it for myself, I always treat myself to a couple of slices of grilled bread with a bit of oil.'

'We just had *ladovreckto*,' Pippo says.

'Ah yes, well with this dish, I smear a little crushed garlic on with the oil.'

'What's this dish called then?' Pippo asks.

'Arakas Kokinistos.'

Vasso organizes the two men as if she were conducting a military campaign and soon has Pippo chopping onions and dill.

'Dill,' she says, 'is the key to this dish, and gives it the flavor.'

Fresh peas are best, apparently, but frozen will do. 'Do not even think about using canned peas though!' she says as she chops garlic. 'You don't have to have the garlic,' she adds, 'but I like it.'

Soon there are amazing smells emanating from the pot on the stove, and Pippo's stomach starts to rumble.

'Of course everyone wants meat these days,' Vasso says, 'but in the old days this would be a main meal, with a little bread perhaps, and some feta.' Mitsos nods his agreement.

'Just keep it on a low heat until you want to eat.' She stirs at the pot and chuckles.

Greek Peas – Arakas Kokkinistos

Ingredients

Exact quantities are NOT important in this recipe, or in most of the recipes in this book. Different cooks will prepare each of the dishes in their own way. I rarely weigh ingredients, and instead judge quantities by eye. These are simple wholesome dishes and not haute cuisine!! Go forth and experiment. Use the instructions as a rough guide.

3 cups (450g) green peas. Frozen peas work fine!

1/3 cup (80g) olive oil

1 cup (150g) chopped onions

2 cloves garlic, minced. Use more garlic if you like!

1/3 cup (5g) chopped fresh dill or to taste

1/3 cup (50g) tomato paste dissolved in 2 cups (470ml) warm water – use 1/4 (40g) if you like less tomato flavor. You can use a tin of tomatoes instead.

1 1/2 tsp salt

1 tsp ground pepper

1 1/2 tbsp crushed, dried Greek oregano

2 cups (470ml) water

Vasso's Instructions

In a large pan, sauté finely chopped onion and garlic in olive oil over low heat until almost translucent, do not let them brown.

Add salt, fresh ground pepper, crushed oregano and fresh dill chopped up with scissors. Stir well and cook on a low heat for 3-4 minutes.

Add the peas, stir and cook for 3-4 minutes. Add tomato paste dissolved in 2 cups of water with an additional 2 cups of water and stir again.

You can add a tin of chopped tomatoes instead, or use fresh tomatoes, as would have been done traditionally. The usual method in Greece is to grate tomatoes when making a dish like this; slice the tomato in two, and grate on a cheese grater holding the tomato skin side out in the palm of your hand. Grate all the way down to the skin (mind your fingers!) and then discard the skin.

Turn up heat and boil for three or four minutes.

Reduce heat and simmer, covered, for 40 minutes.

Serve with crusty bread and slabs of feta.

If there is anything left to reheat tomorrow, add two tablespoons of water for every cup of peas and reheat, covered, on low.

This recipe can be easily scaled to make larger amounts.

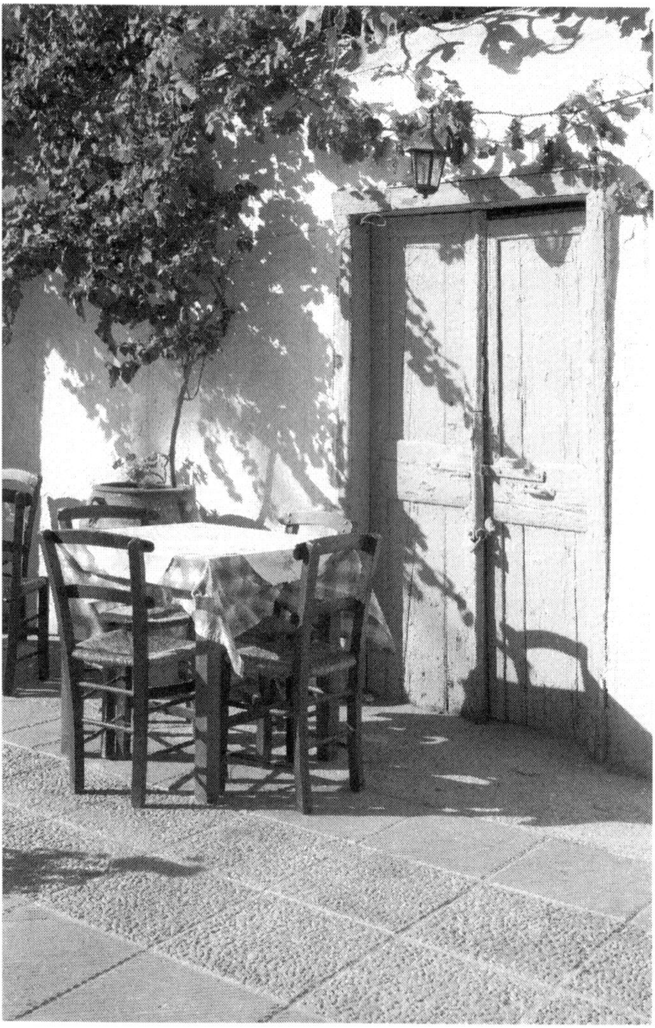

Chapter 4

'Do you know how to make *arakas*?' Pippo asks Mitsos when Vasso is gone.

'Yes, of course. I have been a bachelor most of my life, and I have made more than my fair share of *arakas*. Peas, like onions, are a comparatively fatty vegetable, so they are more satisfying than, say, *horta*, which needs a great deal of olive oil.'

'*Horta*?' Pippo asks.

'*Horta*, hm… I'm afraid I don't know Italian, but if you know any English, I suppose it translates as weeds. If you go up into the mountains, you can collect all sorts of wild leafy greens, and there are more varieties than I could tell you. *Horta* is a general term, but there are different types, such as *vlita*, which have a red stem, and *pikralida*, which is the stem of the dandelion plant. And then there is *radikia*, and *seskoula*, and others. But all this is meaningless unless you see the plant, and anyway, all you do is boil them and add oil, and lemon, and a little salt.'

'So if you have made *arakas* all your life, why did you not just say so to Vasso?'

'She will know I know how to make it, and she knows that Stella knows how to make it, but that was not the point, was it? She wants *arakas* to be her gift to Stella, and to show us her way of doing it. I mean, I don't think I have ever made it with tomato paste and water. I always use fresh tomatoes, but smell it. It smells rich and tasty, no? I reckon that is the tomato paste.'

'Well I am still full from breakfast, so what will you do with it? Give it back to Vasso?'

'Oh good Lord no. I will feed it to the farmers.'

'Who have we here then?' A burly man with a leathered face and neck and forearms strides into the eatery. Pippo stands to one side to let him pass.

'This is Pippo, Italian by birth but Greek by descent. His family are the Alampo. Do you know them?'

'No. Never heard of them, but you are an Alamanos and I am Alanis, and there are plenty of Anastas. Maybe you should choose one of them to be kin to.' And the man slaps his thigh and laughs heartily.

'Pippo, this is Grigoris, one of the many farmers you will meet today.'

'Ciao,' Pippo drawls.

'*Yeia sou*,' Grigoris replies and goes through to the dining room with its four tables. Mitsos follows him through, takes his order, and opens the second door, allowing the sunshine to flood the darkness of the small room, slashing tables and chairs diagonally and making motes dance in its light.

'So he wants our standard. Chicken, chips, lemon sauce.' Mitsos does not rush. He takes a fork and stabs at one of the chickens on the grill. The juices flow out clear. 'If you would be so kind as to pour some chips into the fryer, turn it on there and the timer should be…' He turns a knob on the front fryer. 'Like that.'

'So are you open dawn till dusk?' Pippo asks, pouring in a generous quantity of chips.

'When Stella is here, we are. She normally covers the afternoon when I take a rest. But with her away this week, if there is no one in, I will shut for the afternoon. If you need a break, I understand. The afternoons are hot, and I get sleepy.' He slices up the chicken expertly, with just one hand, and pours lemon sauce over it. The fryer pings just as he has finished, signaling that the chips are ready. 'There you go. Add the chips and take it through.'

The lunch service is a busy one and Pippo is nimble and highly efficient, in a very calm way. He makes light work of the number of plates they serve and rather than letting them mount up as Mitsos and Stella do, he washes them in the sink next to the grill as he collects them up.

By mid-afternoon the place is not only empty but the tables just need a wipe and there is nothing to wash up.

'Well Pippo, my right-hand man, what say we take a break?'

'Sure.' The boy does not seem to mind either way.

'I thought we could pass by Marina at the corner shop and ask her if she knows your people, and we can see if she wants to contribute a dish to Stella's big table.'

'Sure,' Pippo replies, this time with enthusiasm.

Mitsos locks the door to the eatery and blinks in the sunlight.

'I love this time of day, when the village is quiet, when most are sleeping in the heat. Even in the winter it goes quiet, everyone recharging themselves.' He takes a step and steadies himself with his crook.

'This Marina, will she not be sleeping?'

'Ah no. Marina believes the shop should only be shut after eleven at night, and then only if no one drops in for a late-night chat. And she is always open even before the first farmers are awake.' Step, stick, step.

'But she needs to sleep too?'

'Ah, there is her son Petta and his Irini. Between them, they have it covered, as they say. At the moment, Marina is doing the afternoon shift with Irini's baby, who will no longer sleep at this time of day. Here we are. Up three steps.' Mitsos takes the steps one at a time, always leading with his right foot. The area around the door to the shop gives the impression that the contents have exploded out of a space far too small to contain them, and offers a clue about the Aladdin's cave to be found within. Farmers' tools and baking racks hang from the edge of the roof, and Mitsos is obliged to bow his head to avoid hitting them. Next to the door is a rack of fresh vegetables and a crate of empty beer bottles beside it. A string of garlic hangs down the doorframe, and inside, Pippo can clearly see that there is barely room to move for all the goods and foodstuffs on sale.

'That is a fine idea,' Marina exclaims when they have explained their plan. 'So, has anyone said they will make *spanakotiropita*? Because mine is to die for.' She lifts her grandson off her knee and comes out from behind her counter, ducking to avoid the fly whisks that hang from the ceiling.

'No, no one has, Marina,' Mitsos reassures her.

'Well then, you are in luck. Come through.' Her grandson runs before her, down the aisle to the back of the shop, narrowly avoiding knocking over a pair of Wellingtons that are stuffed with an assortment of shepherd crooks that poke out like dead bones. A box of tights, assorted sizes, reduced to sell, are not so fortunate, and Marina bends from her hips, puts the box back on a low shelf as she follows out a narrow back door to the shop into a courtyard.

'You are in luck, as I am just about to make it for Petta and Irini for when they wake.' Marina speaks in a hushed tone. They are in an enclosed space between the back of the shop and the front of Marina's house. A splendid wisteria trails along the top of one wall, hanging heavy with bunches of purple flowers, almost completely obscuring the whitewashed surface. A door in the wall, Mitsos knows, will lead out to the road that goes up past the church and along to the new road that leads down to Stella's little hotel on the beach.

'Look, I was just gathering everything I need so I could put it together out here. Angelos gets so full of energy when I try to keep him in. Don't you, *agapi mou*?' The little boy is busy running a toy car along the soil between the large flagstones, and he does not answer her.

'Do you want something to drink, Mitsos, Pippo?' she offers, and they both shake their heads. 'Right. I will just get the spinach then.' Marina is in and out of the house in a minute, returning with a big pan of blanched spinach and another of sautéed onions.

'You see, I do a little when it's quiet in the shop, and by this time, all I have to do is put it all together, easy as anything. Now, how are you managing, Mitsos, without Stella? Back next week, is she? How is it going for her? Do you think her trip will be useful? Have you met Stella, Pippo? Oh no, of course, you arrived today... From where? Italy you said? Same face, same race.' Whilst she is chattering away, Marina mixes the onions in with the spinach and dumps a block of feta in with it all, crumbling the cheese with a fork and mixing it in with the leaves and the onions.

The surface of the table in the courtyard has been worn smooth by years of use, and the grain is dappled with the sun that is trying to break through the leaves of the lemon trees.

'Oh, goodness. I have forgotten the salt.' Marina stops her chatter and with her slippers slapping on the cobbles, she hurries back inside and out again.

'Oh and the dill!' she exclaims, and she is off again.

'Dill? Again?' Pippo says. 'Does all Greek cooking have dill in it?'

'How old are you?' Marina asks him, grinding pepper into the mixture.

'Eighteen.'

'And you, Mitsos?'

'You know how old I am, Marina! Older than you, that's for sure, but young at heart. Why do you ask?'

'I heard something funny the other day. Someone said "When do you think boys become men?"' She looks up with a grin. 'I will tell you.' Marina starts to giggle. 'A boy becomes a man at forty, if the woman in his life is lucky.' She laughs even more and tears start to run from her eyes. She wipes them away with the back of her hand and tries to stop laughing long enough to deliver the punchline. 'And then a year or two later, they start regressing again into senility…' She can no longer control herself and she is laughing, so much she forgets what she is doing with the pepper grinder and the fork drips pieces of feta onto the flagged floor. 'We cannot win,' she says when she gets herself back in control.

'In that case, I think Stella has missed the moment I was an adult.' Mitsos grins and he looks down at Angelos, who has given up with his toy car and is now teasing a cat with a leaf.

'So, the dill in here?' Pippo asks, offering to add the chopped herb to the bowl.

'Yes.' Marina is still laughing. 'Now, what have I forgotten? There is something important that goes in next. I think it is you two watching! I can usually do this with my eyes shut but today I am forgetting everything.'

'Eggs perhaps?' Mitsos says.

'Ah yes, of course. Eggs. Now, do I have any village eggs left? Let me go and see. Actually Pippo, let me make use of your young energy. In the shop, by the counter, there are two baskets. In the square basket are the eggs from Saros, and in the round basket are the local eggs. Can you bring me two?'

'I thought you kept the eggs by the newspapers,' Mitsos says.

'I do. So what's the deal, who is this boy? I saw him dropped by a bus. Do you know him?'

'Did you tell him to look in the wrong place for the eggs to give yourself time to ask me about him?' Mitsos is amused.

'Well, come on. He will be back soon,' Marina presses.

'Marina, you are terrible! He's just a lad taking a year out, looking for his ancestors.'

'So he just turned up, you don't know him, and now he is helping you with your anniversary dinner?'

'Yes. Why not?'

'What's his name?'

'Alampo.'

'Ah, I've not heard that one, but wasn't there an Alamanos in the next village? He looks Greek, doesn't he?'

'Maybe. Greek or Italian, but with something else mixed in, I think.' He breaks off. 'Ah, did you find them, Pippo? I think Marina sent you on a bit of a hunt.'

'Break them into the bowl then and give them a good stir. There! We are done!' Marina gives the eggs a final beat.

Pippo looks at the bowl dubiously.

'So are you making individual parcels or one big pie?' Mitsos asks.

Spanakopita

Ingredients

For the filling:

2 lb. (1kg) fresh spinach, washed, dried, trimmed, and coarsely chopped

3 Tbs. extra-virgin olive oil

1 bunch scallions (Spring onions) (about 3 oz. / 85g or 10 small), white and light-green parts only, trimmed and finely chopped

2 cups (10 oz. / 280g) crumbled feta cheese

1/2 cup (50g) finely grated Greek kefalotyri cheese or Parmigiano-Reggiano

2 large eggs, lightly beaten

1/2 cup (a good handful) finely chopped fresh dill

1/3 cup (a good handful) finely chopped fresh flat-leaf parsley

1/4 tsp. freshly grated nutmeg

Salt and pepper

For the assembly:

1/3 cup extra-virgin olive oil for brushing; more as needed

Eighteen 9×14-inch sheets frozen filo pastry thawed and at room temperature

2 tsp. whole milk

Directions

Position a rack in the center of the oven and heat the oven to 375°F / 190°C / Gas mark 5

Make the filling: Add a few large handfuls of the spinach to a pan on a medium heat and cook, tossing gently with a fork. As the spinach starts to wilt, add the rest a few handfuls at a time. Cook until all the spinach is wilted and bright green, about 4 minutes. With a slotted spoon, transfer the spinach to a colander set in a sink. Let cool slightly and squeeze with your hands to extract as much of the remaining liquid as you can.

Heat the oil in the pan over medium heat. Add the scallions and cook until soft, about 4 minutes. Stir in the spinach, turn off the heat, and let cool for 5 minutes. Then stir in the cheeses, eggs, dill, parsley, nutmeg, and 1/2 tsp. salt and a little pepper and mix thoroughly.

Assemble the pie: With a pastry brush, lightly coat the bottom and sides of a 9x13x2-inch baking pan with some of the oil. Working quickly, lightly oil one side of a filo pastry sheet and lay it in the pan oiled side up and off center so that it partially covers the bottom and reaches halfway up one long side of the pan (the edge on the bottom of the pan will be about 1 inch from the side). Lightly oil the top of another filo sheet and lay it oiled side up and off center so it reaches halfway up the other long side of the pan. (If your pan has sloped sides, the sheets may be slightly longer than the bottom of the pan; if so, let the excess go up one short side of the pan and then alternate with subsequent sheets.) Repeat this pattern with 4 more filo sheets.

Next, lightly oil the tops of 3 filo sheets and layer them oiled side up and centered in the pan. Spread the filling evenly over the last layer.

Repeat the oiling and layering of the remaining 9 filo sheets over the filling in the same way you layered the previous 9. With the oiled bristles of the pastry brush, push the edges of the filo sheets down around the sides of the pan to enclose the filling completely.

With a sharp knife, score the top filo layer into rectangles, being careful not to cut all the way through to the filling. Using the same pastry brush, brush the milk along all the score marks (this will keep the filo from flaking up along the edges of the squares). Bake the spanakopita until the top crust is golden brown, 35 to 45 minutes. Let cool until just warm. Cut out the rectangles carefully along the score marks and serve.

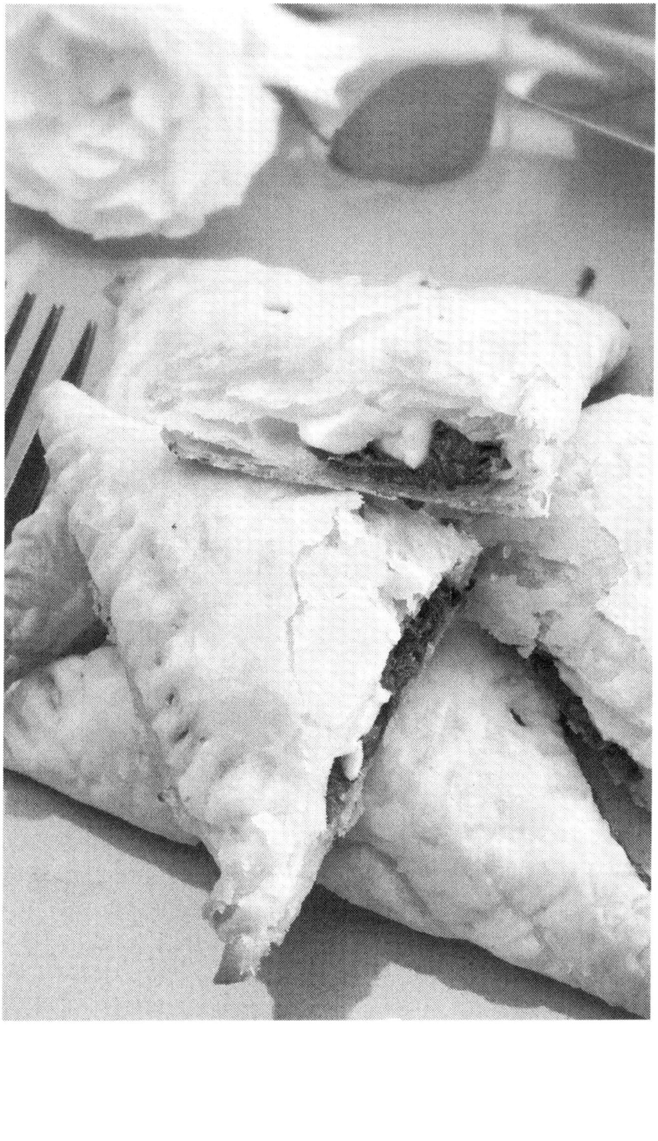

Chapter 5

Marina invites them both to eat with her family but Pippo is still full and Mitsos says he has an errand to run before Stella gets back.

'Better to do it now and have it done,' he says.

The village square is quiet; most people are in their homes. The villagers do not visit each other at this time of day. They sleep or rest in the heat.

'I have to take the van just along the road there.' Mitsos points first at a battered vehicle which is parked on the square and then up the road that runs past the kafenio. 'Stella is complaining that the brakes are not working, although they seem fine to me.'

They climb in the truck and Pippo notices that a few adjustments have been made so Mitsos can drive it. It is automatic for a start, and a knob has been added to the steering wheel so Mitsos can steer easily with one hand. The journey is short, and before they have really got going, the vehicle is manoeuvred into a yard in front of a traditional whitewashed house with several cars parked in front, up and down the road in both directions. On the far side of the yard, in front of the cottage but beyond the wall, are orange groves. On the near side of the yard, a man dressed in overalls sits in the shade of a lemon tree that hangs heavy with fruit. A sound of voices chatting comes from around the side of the whitewashed stone cottage.

'*Yeia sou*, Aleko,' Mitsos greets the man. 'Aleko, Pippo.' He makes the introduction.

'Ah, you caught me taking a break! The wife is round the side with the children. Come, let's go round and see them.' He says all this with a heavy, outward breath.

'Ah Mitsos, are you still abandoned or is Stella back yet?' Aleko's wife is a good-looking woman with dark hair tied back in a ponytail that sits between her fine shoulder blades.

'Athena, this is Pippo,' says Mitsos. Pippo tries to concentrate on the introduction but he cannot keep his eyes off a girl around his age with shiny dark blond hair and olive skin. She is mixing something in a bowl on a large wooden table set in the shade of a pergola that is bending under the weight of a gnarled old vine.

'And that is Eva, Aleko and Athena's eldest daughter,' Mitsos says, and Pippo feels his cheeks on fire. He must have made his staring too obvious.

'Yes, our fourth.' Athena says. 'Three boys older than her, then we got two girls, then another boy, and another girl, and the youngest is another boy, six months old now.' She looks lovingly into a basket that Pippo had presumed was washing, but only for a moment, as he cannot take his eyes from Eva.

'So Mitso, have you brought the truck finally?' Aleko asks and the two of them wander back around to where they left the vehicle. Athena goes inside with the baby in the basket.

'It's feeding time,' she mutters.

Pippo moves closer to Eva in pretence of being interested in what she is doing.

'Do you know that there is something called mad honey?' Eva says, taking a small spoonful of sticky fluid from a jar. 'Don't worry; this is not mad honey. No, the mad honey comes from Turkey. The farmers take their hives to fields bordered by rhododendrons and this gives the honey some property that makes you feel drunk when you eat it, they say. It's some toxin in the rhododendron flowers, and too much and your blood pressure drops and it is dangerous.' She holds the small spoon right up to Pippo's mouth. He tentatively puts out his tongue to taste. Her eyes watch his mouth's every move. For some reason, Pippo feels excited by this.

'Leave him alone.' A boy as tall as himself, clearly related to Eva, strides from around the side of the house and in through the back door.

'Get lost!' Eva calls after him but her neck and cheeks flush and she flings the spoon onto the table. Pippo notices there are flecks of red in her hair and her skin has just a touch of ginger.

'Is it usual to be blond and Greek?' he asks her.

'They say it's a throwback.' She is still glaring into the doorway after her brother. 'You know before we mixed with the Arabs, the Greeks were blond, they say. Where are you from? You are not Greek.'

'I am Italian, but four generations ago, one of my ancestors came from around here. My uncle used to relate tales his grandfather would tell from around these parts.'

'This village?' She looks up with interest from the bowl of nuts she is grinding .

'Well, he said it was a village outside of Saros that had a small hill topped with trees, so my guess is it is this one. Of course, trees may have come and gone since then.'

'I can't think of another village with a hill though.' For a moment she meets his eyes. Her irises are blue but her lashes are dark, clustered tightly. He is mesmerised. 'So, four generations ago, eh?' She brings him back to focus.

'Yes. He would talk about Big Stantos, big as a bear, who would wrestle for money and would drink a bottle of whiskey down straight.'

'Eva, Constantinos won't let me have my doll.' A child appears from under the table. With a dip of his head, Pippo spies two more children and a dog under the table. Eva takes no notice, and there is a little scuffling and the voice comes again. 'He's given me it now,' it announces, as if this is a regular procedure.

Pippo returns his attention to Eva, who is screwing the lid back on the jar of honey.

'What are you making?'

'Baklava.'

'Isn't it tricky? I heard it was difficult to make.'

'No, it's easy. All you need is time—and the pressure of seven brothers and sisters who want to eat it!' She laughs at this, throwing her head back, elongating her neck, her hair falling about her shoulders. She has her mama's bone structure. At some point, it looks as if she tried to cut her hair herself, as she has the tiniest of curls along the top of her forehead, all different lengths. It softens her high brow and Pippo does not think he has ever seen anything so perfect.

'I like making it, especially painting on the butter and layering the filo pastry.' She holds a pan in one hand and a brush in the other, painting the baking dish, smearing all the sides. 'I think you are meant to use a knife to cut the pastry but I always use scissors, and I use the bits I cut off to make shapes with and decorate the top.'

Pippo pretends to be interested and tries to think of something to say, but he feels as if his mouth has dried. 'Oh,' he manages at last. 'Mitsos is going to surprise Stella with a big get-together with food.' The words sound awkward and then he realises he does not have the authority to invite her, but he has started now; he will have to make it right with Mitsos later.

'She is always cooking.' Eva puts in another layer of filo pastry and begins painting again with the melted butter from the pan.

'Mitsos is asking everyone to make a dish and bring it, as a present.'

'Oh, I will make a baklava for her!' Eva says, sprinkling nuts over the pastry and then adding another layer of filo. Pippo picks up the butter brush absentmindedly just at the same moment as Eva reaches out for it. Their hands touch and their eyes meet just as the brother returns from outside. Hands on his hips, his lips tighten to a line and he stares with hard eyes at Pippo.

Baklava

Here's an easy recipe for mouth-watering baklava!

For the syrup:

It's best to make the syrup in advance as it needs to cool to room temperature.

5 cups (1.25l) cold water

3 cups (600g) caster or granulated sugar

6 cinnamon sticks

5 whole cloves (To taste but do not omit)

Put all the ingredients in a pan, bring to the boil, then allow to simmer and thicken. The syrup will thicken more once cool.

Remove the cinnamon sticks and cloves once the syrup has cooled to room temperature.

Next, gather together:

A 13 x 9 in tapsi (oven dish)

1 lb (450g) butter

2 lb (900g) filo pastry

1 lb (450g) coarsely ground walnuts (Mitsos still has some whole from last year)

¼ cup (35g) cinnamon

½ cup (100g) caster or granulated sugar

Directions

In a bowl, Combine the walnuts, sugar, cinnamon and mix well.

Melt the butter. Grease the inside of the tapsi using a butter brush.

Cover the bottom with two layers of filo pastry. Be sure to butter each well, then cover the bottom and each side allowing the pasty to hang over (Use four sheets, one for each side).

Layer over the bottom a third of the walnut mixture then drizzle butter over the top of that.

Cover with another layer of filo pastry and crumple this layer to create air pockets. This will help make the baklava light.

Next cover the entire layer with drizzled butter.

Now layer another third of the walnut mix and again drizzle with butter.

Repeat with scrunched filo pastry and more butter. Be generous!

The last stage is to fold over the sheets you laid over the sides when you started, overlapping them, and covering each with butter. Add six smooth layers of filo pastry to finish off, buttering each as you lay it.

It is best to score your cuts into the top at this stage but do not cut all the way through. Score bite-sized pieces.

You can either bring it to me at the bakery and I will cook it, or if you wish to do it at home set the oven to 325 Fahrenheit / 160 Celsius / Gas 3 and bake for 45 minutes. Then raise the temperature to 350 Fahrenheit / 180 Celsius / Gas 4 and bake till golden brown – another 15 to 30 minutes depending on your oven. If it cooks longer than this you may find it a little dry.

As soon as the baklava is done you should take it out of the oven and pour the (room temperature) syrup evenly over the top. The syrup will absorb better into the baklava if it is at room temperature.

Let the baklava set for at least 4 hours, then cut and enjoy.

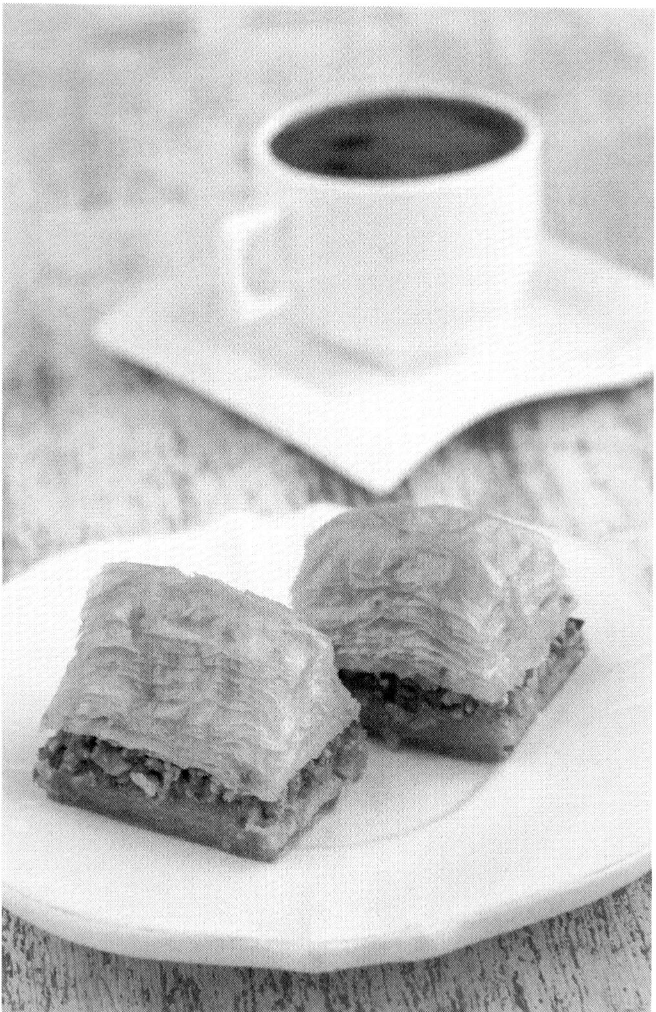

Chapter 6

Pippo stands his ground and stares back, and finally the brother tuts his disapproval and walks away, around the corner to the front of the cottage. It is a victory, and Pippo's spine straightens. He steps closer to Eva.

'You wanna go into town with me? We can go get coffee somewhere or something…' Pippo is a little taken aback at his bold words, and his heart beats faster, but she is so comfortable to be with, so easy on the eye, that the chance to get to know her better is worth risking making a fool of himself.

'Oh!' The gasp is slightly high-pitched. He has caught her off-guard.

'Nothing heavy,' he declares quickly. The sun catches the blond in her hair. He feels hypnotised, slightly drunk, as if she has fed him mad honey.

'Well, obviously today I am busy.' She points at the baklava, and then swats half-heartedly at a bee. 'But I do have to go to the market very early tomorrow. Perhaps we will bump into each other there, and maybe we will be thirsty… Then it would be very natural to go for something to drink.' Eva's voice is unsteady and she looks down, not meeting his eye. Pippo is encouraged, but before he can reply, the brother returns, standing by the table with his feet apart and his hands folded over his chest, glaring. There is no blond in him at all; he is all dark—dark hair, dark eyebrows, dark skin, dark mood.

'I'd best go help Mitsos.' Pippo puts his hands in the front pockets of his jeans and flicks his head back to get his curls out of his eyes. 'See you.' He makes a point of looking directly at Eva.

'See you.' Her eyes are on her baklava and her brother moves a step closer to her, as if to claim her. Pippo is not sure exactly what they have agreed.

'You must be pleased to find some people your own age?' Mitsos says as Pippo returns to him and the truck. Aleko is under the lemon tree, noisily sorting through a box of tools. He dumps them on the floor with a grunt and the leaves above his head rustle. Pippo looks up to see a bird breaking free to fly away across the endless blue sky.

'I was wondering if you needed me tomorrow morning?' Pippo asks Mitsos.

'Have you found something better to do?' Mitsos smiles.

'I just fancy going into Saros to see the market. It is tomorrow, isn't it?'

'Actually, that's a good point. I need to go to into Saros for charcoal, so I see no reason why we cannot go to the market. As long as we go early, I can get back in time.'

They are back at the eatery in plenty of time to prepare for the evening. Pippo uses the last of the charcoal on the grill as Mitsos stuffs paper napkins into holders on each table. The evening is not particularly busy and Mitsos suggests they close early.

'Where are you staying?' he asks, pulling the door to, and Pippo realises he has not given a thought to the question of where he might sleep. He has little money and besides, if he sleeps on the beach, it won't be the first time. He answers with a non-committal shrug.

'From my house, up on that hill,' Mitsos points with his keys, 'I get to see the sunset over the sea to the west. I also play a mean game of tavli.'

He is not wrong. After five games, Pippo declares Mitsos unbeatable.

'Do you play chess?' he asks.

'Never quite got on with chess.' And so they sit looking at the stars in companionable silence until Mitsos yawns, stretching his one arm heavenwards. 'You know, I think I will turn in. The sheets for the day bed are in the drawers underneath. You can manage?'

'Yes, of course. Thank you.' It seems the most natural thing in the world to stay.

The following day is glorious, not a cloud in the sky, an even blue stretching from the mountains behind the house all the way to the horizon, where the sun's disc is just breaking above the surface of the sea. Pippo wakes with excitement.

'Would you like me to go and get the truck for you, save you the walk down?' Mitsos seems in no hurry to leave the house.

'No, no. The walk will do me good.' It seems to take him forever to put on his boots. Pippo jiggles nervously from foot to foot and is tempted to offer to help, but holds his tongue and reaches for the old man's crook, thrusting it towards him once he is on his feet. Pippo leads the way along the track that leads from the cottage onto the lane and into the village. The truck is ready and waiting outside Aleko's, but there is no sign of Eva. Is she in town already, or still inside the house? Pippo cannot muster the confidence to ask Aleko and he agonises, unsure whether to encourage Mitsos to linger at the house or hurry him to the market.

When they do set off, the truck trundles and jostles them along the potholed road towards Saros. The atmosphere at the market is reminiscent of those in Italy, but different somehow. There is an easy cheerfulness, as if everyone knows everyone, and jovial conversations are being had between stall holders and shoppers with no pressure to buy or make a sale.

One of the roads off the main junction in Saros has been closed off for the market, and stalls are lined up on either side, with makeshift canvas awnings meeting in the middle. Where they don't meet, extra canvas has been introduced to keep the sun's heat from both shoppers and produce. Shafts of light still pierce to the ground through gaps that have been missed, like randomly placed spotlights.

Pippo finds his nostrils assaulted, first with the tang of citrus, and then a cacophony of herbs. Earthy smells drift from newly plucked potatoes and beetroot and a sweet aroma from a stall laden with dried figs and dates.

'So, I only need to get a bag of charcoal.' Mitsos points at a hardware shop across the road in front of which, taking up most of the pavement, is a selection of ladders, cement mixers, and soil cultivators. 'But as we are here, I think I will buy the ingredients for *melitzanosalata*. We can have it for our lunch, or maybe dinner. All we need is a couple of aubergines, onions… I have garlic, some tomatoes, and the rest of the ingredients. Olive oil, vinegar, seasoning I also have. Oh, we need green peppers. There…' He stops at a stall. 'Look at those tomatoes.' Mitsos points, but Pippo's mind is not on the fruit and vegetables. Eva must be somewhere. 'Smell that one.' Mitsos holds a tomato under Pippo's nose.

'Great,' Pippo replies absently, still searching the faces in the crowd. There, a few stalls on, between a woman clad in black and a man in a pale blue shirt, he spots a blue dress, a lean neck, pale hair piled up, and he scoots off, dodging old ladies and shopping trolleys. When he reaches her and taps on her shoulder, an expectant grin on his face, he is not only disappointed but slightly shocked to find it is a woman in her mid-thirties, or maybe even older, and not Eva at all. 'Sorry,' he mutters.

'Who was that?' Mitsos asks with a twinkle in his eye.

'Oh, just I thought I knew…' Pippo can hear how lame he sounds.

'But you don't know anybody here?'

Pippo senses Mitsos is teasing him.

'Did you want garlic?'

'No, I have garlic at home. So who did you think she was exactly?'

'Green peppers. You said you needed green peppers.' Pippo picks up a large red pepper and holds it for Mitsos to smell. This distraction works—the old man seems to take delight in the textures and smells of all that is on offer, and they continue to explore the market together.

A clock somewhere towards the centre of town strikes twelve.

'We cannot have been that long, can we?' Mitsos says.

'I guess we have.' Pippo buys a bag of almonds and offers them to Mitsos.

'Well, I suggest we grab a bite to eat here and then when we get back, we can concentrate on our customers. What do you say?' There is a youthful energy in Mitsos's voice that is at odds with his appearance, and Pippo wonders what sort of man he was before his accident. It would actually make more sense to go back and get the grill going, eat as they wait for it to heat, but Mitsos is clearly enjoying himself and the novelty of being in town.

'That sounds like a great idea.' Pippo has resigned himself to not meeting Eva after all, but he scans the faces under the awnings again as they turn to leave, just in case. There is no sign of Eva—maybe they did not have a date after all. A sense of disappointment begins to fill him; the energy of expectation leaves his limbs. If he is honest, he doesn't care if they get back or stay in Saros.

With their purchases deposited in the van, they leave the market, heading for the old town between sandy-orange stone buildings. There seems to be a Venetian influence here and Pippo suddenly feels more at home. Instead of the washing strung between the buildings that he half expects, there are garlands of bougainvillea which are delightful in the purple and pink, but they do not touch his heart as he not only feels the disappointment of not meeting Eva, but now he is also thinking about his mama back in Italy.

Mitsos leads the way to a large square, paved with smooth marble and with trees dotted for shade and cafés around the edges offering cool drinks and comfortable chairs. Mitsos heads straight for the far corner, where tables are arranged in the shade of an ancient plane tree. The chairs here are made of cane work with cushions for comfort. There are also electric fans propped between the tables which not only spin to cool the air but also spray a mist of water that cancels out the heat.

'Here looks good.' Mitsos sits, propping his crook against the iron railings that encirle the trunk of the massive plane tree. A waiter is there before Pippo has even had a chance to sit down.

The waiter rattles out a greeting at such a speed that Pippo is suddenly aware that Mitsos has been speaking very slowly and clearly all the time they have been together.

'Sorry?'

'What would you like?' the waiter repeats, this time in fluent Italian, which makes Pippo smile but also twists his heart just a little, reminding him he is a long way from home. He takes his money from his front pocket and spreads it on the table top.

'Is that all you have you have with you?' Mitsos asks, his shock apparent.

'Uh huh!'

'But you have your ticket back, yes?'

'Can I get you anything?' the waiter jiggles change in his pocket.

'Oh yes. Coffee?' Mitsos says. Pippo nods. 'Frappe.'

'Sweet, please,' Pippo adds and the waiter marches off, scribbling on his notepad.

Mitsos watches the children kicking a ball about in the centre of the square. Their game comes to a sudden halt as a toddler escapes his mama's arms and makes for a cloud of translucent bubbles that are being blown by a very large man, also in the centre of the square. His bulk swamps a rickety table next to him, on which he has arranged his bottles of bubble mixture. He is surrounded by a crowd of excited children, all leaping for his bubbles, and by more bottles of bubble mixture that stand around him ready to be sold, like soldiers to attention. He appears to double as one of the goalposts for the football game; a child's rucksack marks the other. A little apart from the bubble man stands a gyspy holding an umbrella of brightly coloured balloons that threaten to lift her off the ground, there are so many! Heavy skirts keep her anchored to the ground.

Something touches Pippos's leg and he looks down to find a cat looking back up at him, smiling and purring. Pippo strokes it and ruffles the fur behind its ears. Mitsos watches Pippo giving the cat pleasure, beginning to wonder about this boy with no luggage and no money. Has he really taken a year out from college? He looks too young to have left school. Maybe he is a runaway. If Stella was here, she would have found out his whole story already and then she would tuck him under her small wing and keep him there until he wriggled free. Stella would have made a wonderful mama.

Pippo is looking at the menu.

'This cafe does not make much food, but it has snacks, chips, and pizzas, that sort of thing.' Mitsos says. 'I'll tell you what though,' he continues, 'it is the best place in all of Saros for *pantzaria* with *skordalia*.' Mitsos leans his weight back in his chair, the sun warming his face where it breaks through the leaves of the plane tree.

'I'm afraid I don't think my Greek's good enough.'

'Well, you know *skordo*, which means garlic?' Pippo nods.

'And *pantzaria* is, how do they say in...'

The waiter is there with the drinks. '*Barbabietola rossa*. Beetroot,' he says with a wide grin. He sets the drinks on their table and spins the empty tray on one finger. 'It's very good. You want some?'

Melitzanosalata

Aubergine / eggplant salad dishes can be found in multiple cultures across the world including Argentina, Ethiopia, Spain, Turkey, and Armenia. Melitzanosalata is the Greek version, and it's delicious!

Ingredients

3 to 4 (long type) aubergines / eggplants

1 small grated onion

1 to 2 cloves crushed garlic

1 large, peeled and chopped tomato

¾ / 180ml cup olive oil

1 tablespoon vinegar

Salt

Pepper

Black olives for garnishing

Green peppers for garnishing

Directions

Wash the aubergines / eggplants, place in a baking pan and bake in a moderate oven (about 180-190 Celsius, 325 – 350 Fahrenheit / Gas mark 4) - for about one hour or until soft. Allow the skin to turn black so as to give a smoky flavour. Skin the aubergines / eggplants while still hot and chop into small pieces. Continue chopping while slowly adding the onion, garlic, tomatoes, oil, vinegar, salt and pepper.

If you want you can use a blender to get a smooth dip, or leave it chunky.

Put in a salad bowl, and garnish with olives and green pepper rings.

Feel free to experiment – there are many different versions of this dish, and I've even tried one with chopped walnuts in it…

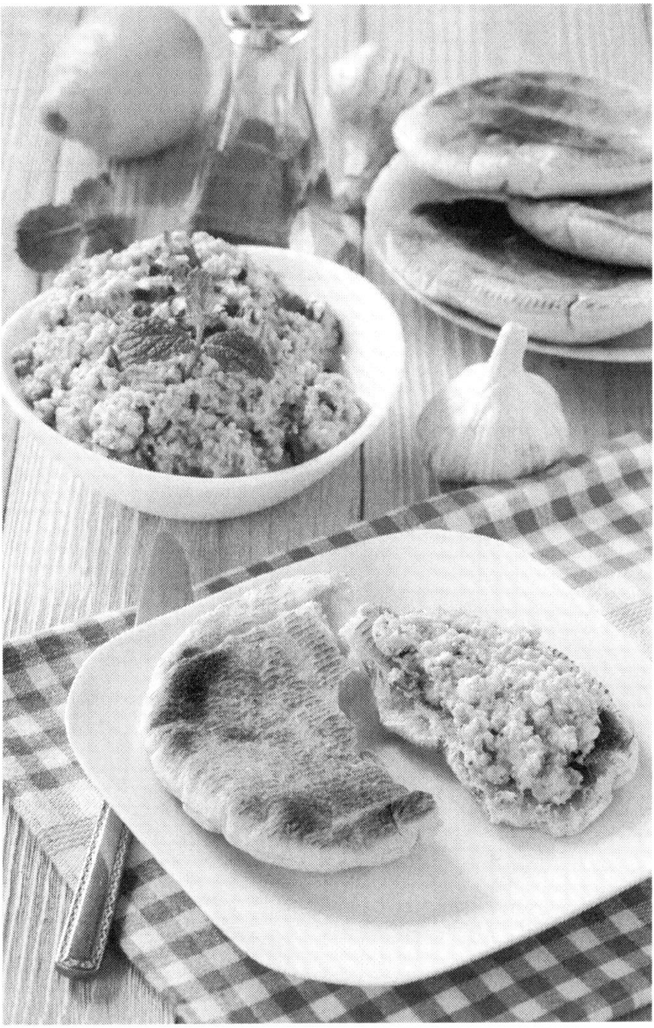

Pantzaria Skordalia – Beetroot with Garlic Dip

This is a dish I will often order if I eat out at a taverna in Greece.It's one of the many vegetable based dishes that are common in Greece but don't seem to make it onto the menus of Greek restaurants abroad. A shame, because to me these are the most 'Greek' choices… The quantities shown here will serve approximately 6 – 8.

Ingredients

2lbs / 900g beets, washed

3tablespoons garlic, minced

1⁄2cup / 120ml olive oil

1⁄2cup / 120ml red wine vinegar

salt and pepper

garlic sauce

4potatoes, washed but unpeeled

3tablespoons garlic, minced

1cup / 240ml olive oil

1⁄3cup / 80ml white wine vinegar (or plain white vinegar)

1teaspoon salt

1⁄4teaspoon pepper

Directions

Wash beets and cut off greens. Wash and cook the greens by boiling in water, or they can be sautéed with a little olive oil.

Wrap beets in foil and place in a sheet pan and bake in a 350 degree / 180 Celsius / Gas 4 oven for 1 hour. You can bake the garlic too if you prefer it to raw.

Test with knife for soft center.

Let cool slightly. Unwrap and peel beets. Cut into quarters or slice.

Place in a bowl and add garlic, olive oil, vinegar.

Add the salt and pepper to taste.

Serve warm or cold.

Can be made 1-2 days ahead of time.

An alternative to baking is to boil the beets, allow to cool then peel off the skin and slice.

Garlic Sauce

Place unpeeled potatoes in small pot and bring to a boil. Reduce heat to cook until ready. Test with knife for soft center.

When cooled slightly, peel. Place potatoes and garlic in medium bowl and mash.

Add vinegar, salt and pepper.

Blend thoroughly.

Can be served at room temperature or cold.

Can be made ahead 1-2 days.

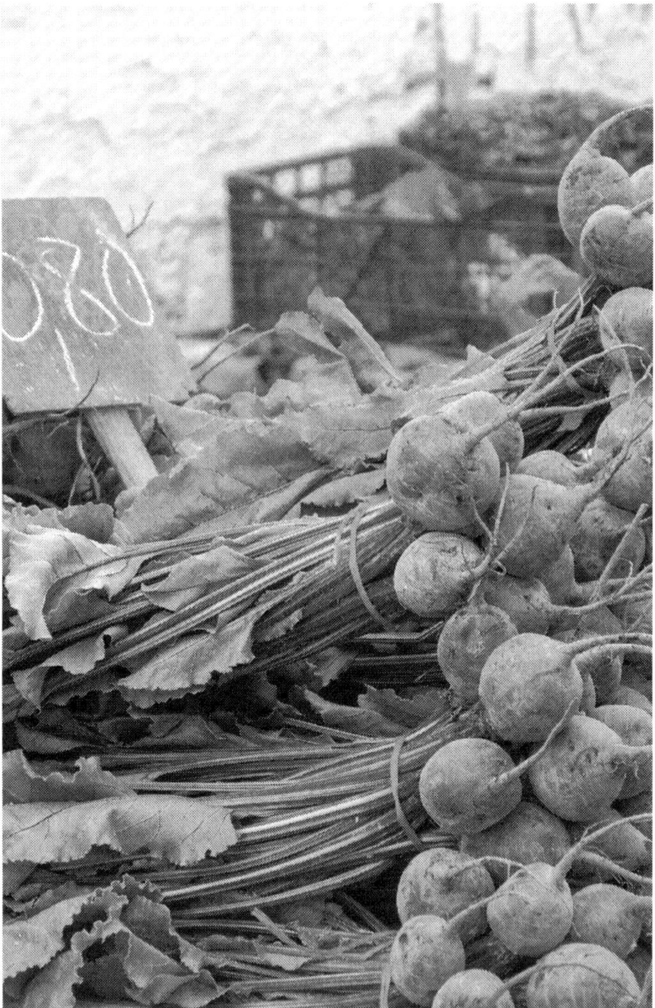

Chapter 7

The food was good, the conversation was easy and, as they approached the outskirts of the village, Pippo had the strangest feeling that he was returning home. This was obviously ridiculous but it had something to do with the down-to-earth nature of the people he has met and their friendly attitudes, which are at odds with Forte de Marmi, which is all high walls and snobby attitudes, close friends excepted. But even his closest friends seem inordinately concerned with their crazily expensive trainers and designer hoodies. He pulls his t-shirt down at the front. He should have brought at least a change of shirt. He surreptitiously sniffs at his armpit as he washes the last of the lunch plates in the eatery. He has spent more time than was strictly necessary collecting and washing them one table at a time. But there was no choice as, since they got back to the village, he has felt like a lizard on hot sand, shifting his weight from foot to foot, expending energy needlessly to try to calm thoughts of Eva and whether she was just playing with him when she said she would meet him at the market.

'You have the energy to burn today,' Mitsos observes. 'Perhaps a quick walk around the village might help. Oh, and if you see Aleko, you could let him know the truck is fine and thank him for me. I would much appreciate that.'

Pippo feels like a dog let off the leash as his legs propel him across the square. He hears Mitsos chuckle as he skips out of the eatery, and Vasso waves cheerfully from the kiosk. Theo from the *kafenio* gives him a nod in recognition, but none of these things matter; there is only one place he needs to go, and he must go directly or he will lose his nerve.

It is not far to the garage, but a sweat has broken out on his forehead by the time he gets there. He puts his hands on his knees to catch his breath and peers under his curls at the house. The shutters are closed and there is no sign of life. The church clock begins to chime three, reminding him that it is time for siesta, and not for visiting. But it was in the afternoon that Mitsos brought the truck to Aleko, so maybe… Voices from around the side of the house make up his mind. Aleko's wife is hanging washing in the yard and talking to her laundry basket, which gurgles back at her.

'Why are you on the other side of the wall?' she says when she sees Pippo. 'Come in.'

'I was just wondering if Eva is around.' He makes no move to go into the yard.

'Ah, Eva is it? Well, well, as it happens, I know where she is.' She puts down her empty washing basket and picks up the basket with her baby. 'Please come in. Let's not talk over the wall.' She turns towards the house and Pippo feels his heartbeat increase. It's partly at the thought of seeing Eva, but he is also nervous at the prospect of meeting one of her brothers.

He tries to look casual as he walks across the yard to the back door of the house, letting his legs swing with each step, hands in his pockets, head bowed and feet scuffing the concrete. The whitewash is flaking off around the door of the cottage, showing the stones behind and the mud mortar between them which betray the building's age. He puts out his hand unconsciously to pick at it.

'Come in,' Eva's mama calls, and with tentative steps he walks along a tiled corridor through to the kitchen. It is a bright room in which the window and another door open onto the rear of the yard that is flanked by orange trees. The walls and furniture are all white, the top of the table scrubbed clean, and it is tidier than one would expect with so many children in the house. His own mother struggles to manage, and there is only him.

'I don't mean to disturb you.' There is no sign of Eva's brother, and no sounds in the house or movement in the yard.

'I only have the little one. The young ones are still at school and the big boys are at work. I suppose I should call them men. They are about your age ' She laughs.

Pippo wants to ask where Eva is, but as he has already mentioned her name, he feels that he would be pressing the point. All over the clean table are various ingredients, as if she has been shopping and unloaded the bag on the table.

She sees him looking at the mountain of produce.

'With so many children, I am permanently cooking or washing!' Her face lights up as if she could think of nothing better to do with her time.

'You've heard of Mitsos' plan for Stella?' he says.

'Oh yes! I understand Eva is making baklava. So today I will make *revikokeftedes* and *kolokithokeftedes*. They are good for the children, filling, and easy to make. And everyone loves them!'

Pippo's expression is blank.

'They're just like meatballs but without the expense of the meat. *Revithokeftedes* are made from chickpeas and *kolokithokeftedes* from courgettes. But you would not believe it was courgette. They are so rich, so tasty, and the children say I never make enough. I want to make them for Stella because I use limes in mine, and no one else does that.'

'That does sound amazing, and different… Did you say Eva was coming back…?' He knows he sounds clumsy but his eagerness got the better of him.

'Yes, sorry. I forgot you were looking for Eva. I am quite easy-going. After all, I was young once too. But in case you haven't have already noticed, her brothers and, indeed, her father, are not so open-minded. Her brothers are quite protective…' She rolls her eyes as if this is all beyond her control.

'Okay…' She exhales a lungful of air, as if she has come to a difficult decision. 'Eva is getting an English lesson round at Juliet's house.'

She comes around the table, takes him by the arm, and leads him outside into the yard and points to the square. 'Left from there, and then right.'

It is all the information he needs, and he is about to set off.

'Wait! You don't need an excuse, but I am going to give you one anyway.' She goes indoors and comes back with a chiffon scarf. 'This is Juliet's, and if you could return it for me, I would be very grateful.' And then she gives him a little push and a smile.

He does not run this time, but his pace is brisk despite the heat. Theo, the man who runs the kafenio, nods as he passes, and it feels almost as if he belongs. He nods back and makes a mental note to take Mitsos there for an ouzo. That would be a good way to end the evening and show his appreciation for the old man's hospitality, but right now he must find Eva. Her mama's directions lead him up a narrow lane, at the end of which is a metal gate with an arch of flowers over it.

Revithokeftedes (Chick Pea Patties)

Ingredients

400g/14 ounces / 2.5 cups boiled chickpeas (200-250g/ 7-8 ounces raw)

4 cloves of garlic

1 red onion

1 tbsp fresh parsley, chopped

2 tsps cumin

2 tsps powdered coriander

2 tbsps flour

Salt and freshly ground pepper

Oil for frying

For the yoghurt sauce

200g yogurt (7 ounces) / just under 1 full cup

juice of half a lemon

1.5 tbsp olive oil

1 tbsp cold water

1 tbsp fresh dill, finely chopped

1 tbsp fresh spearmint finely chopped

Salt

Directions

Soak the chickpeas in a large bowl filled with water and a pinch of salt for about 6 hours, or overnight. Drain and place them into a large pan, filled with water and boil for 40-60 minutes, until soft. When done, drain them into a colander. If using tinned chick peas, which are already boiled of course, you can skip this step.

Place the chick peas on paper towel on a large tray and let them dry out for about an hour. It is very important that they dry out completely.

In the meantime, finely chop the onions and garlic. Place a pan into medium heat, add 2 tbsps of olive oil and sauté, until tender.

Use a food processor to mix all the ingredients together. Add the boiled chickpeas, the sautéed onions and garlic, along with the cumin and coriander and mix. Open the food processor, blend the mixture with a spoon and mix again. Repeat 2-3 times, until all the ingredients are combined. This should take 2-3 minutes.

Into a large bowl, add the chopped parsley, 2 tbsps of flour and the chickpea mixture. Season well with salt and pepper and mix well, squeezing the ingredients with your hands, until combined. Roll the mixture into balls.

Fry the balls in a very hot oil, until nicely colored on all sides. Place them on paper towel, to absorb the extra oil. For a healthier version, bake them in preheated oven at 180C for about 25 minutes. Brush the bottom of the baking tray and the top of the balls with some olive oil. Halfway through cooking time, flip the balls and put back in the oven.

To prepare the sauce, combine all the ingredients until smooth and creamy.

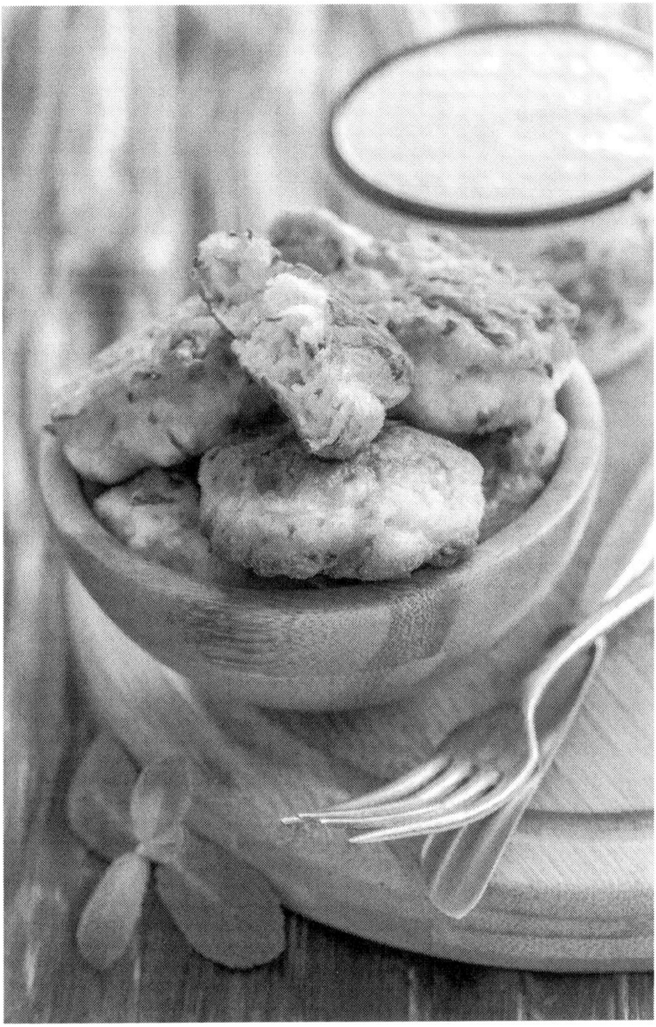

Kolokithokeftedes - Courgette Fritters

Ingredients

For Fritters:

6 large courgettes / zucchini

6 tablespoons dill, chopped

1 bunch (about 8) scallions (spring onions), white and light green parts finely chopped

1/2 teaspoon nutmeg

1 1/2 cups crumbled feta

4 large eggs, lightly beaten

1 cup / 140g plain flour (plus more if needed)

Salt and pepper

4 tablespoons olive oil

For Tzatziki:

2 cups / 500g / 18oz Greek yogurt

1 clove of garlic, minced

1/2 cup / 75g / 2.5oz peeled, grated cucumber

1 teaspoon red wine vinegar or lemon juice

1 tablespoon extra virgin olive oil

Salt and pepper

Directions

Tzatziki: Using a clean tea towel or by pressing in to a sieve, squeeze excess moisture from the grated cucumber. In a small bowl, mix yogurt, garlic, cucumber and vinegar or lemon juice. Stir in olive oil. Add salt and pepper to taste.

Fritters: Lay out a layer of paper towels and spread out grated courgette / zucchini. Sprinkle courgette / zucchini with salt and let sit for at least thirty minutes and up to an hour. Squeeze out all excess moisture from courgette / zucchini.

Put drained courgette / zucchini in a large bowl with dill, scallions, nutmeg, and feta. Mix to combine. Stir in eggs. Season with salt and pepper. Stir in flour until dough comes together, adding slightly more flour if dough is too wet to form patties. Form dough into 3-4 inch patties.

Heat olive oil in a large skillet over medium high heat. Fry patties until golden brown on both sides and cooked through but still moist, about 2-3 minutes per side. Serve hot with tzatziki alongside.

Chapter 8

There is a sense of order about the house at the end of the lane, as though great pains have been taken over its upkeep, but without making it look too new or shiny. The result is traditional but cared for, with the emphasis on comfort. At one end of the terrace is a sagging sofa, and at the other, a table and four chairs. Between these, hanging from the pergola that extends the full length of the terrace, are two canvas chairs that reach nearly to the ground. A grape vine covers the pergola, sinewy tendrils reaching down in places, creating shade. It looks cool and inviting. The house is freshly whitewashed, with a dark orange tiled roof. Vibrant pink and scarlet dots of colour—heads of geranium—stand tall out of pots that have been painted a deep rich blue, a shocking contrast. There is no sign of any people. Pippo taps on the gate but it seems unlikely he could be heard inside. He taps again, harder this time, and the gate swings open and a black and white cat runs, tail up, to greet him. But still there is no sign of life from the house.

With the cat in his arms, he crunches across the gravel and steps up onto the terrace. Inside, he can hear voices so he knocks on the open door.

'Now who can that be?' a voice says very precisely in English.

'I do not know.' The reply is also in English, but strongly accented.

'We must go and see.' Pippo smiles at the forced conversation and the teacher's imagination in using his arrival to extend the lesson. English was not his best subject at school but he joins in anyway.

'I am a stranger in these lands.' He chuckles to himself. 'I am a stranger in these lands looking for care and warmth. I have come many miles to find the place I belong, where I will be treated well.' Perhaps he has gone over the top, but he finds his own ridiculousness amusing.

'Who on earth is that?' The English voice now sounds genuine.

'I think it is Italian boy I meeting yesterday,' Eva says in stuttering English.

'Oh, well, he must come in,' and a tall blonde woman appears at the door. Her smile is warm and welcoming and she stands to one side to let him through.

'Juliet, this is Pippo from Italy,' Eva introduces him.

'I'm very pleased to meet you, Pippo.' Juliet is talking in her teacher's voice again, and Pippo is glad that the focus is not directed at him.

'I am very pleased to meet you too.'

'Today, Pippo, we are practicing words we use around the kitchen.' Juliet is by the sink now with a knife in one hand. 'Today I am making artichoke stew.' She holds up an artichoke. 'My neighbour taught me how to make it. Do you like stew?'

'I like stew a lot,' Eva answers.

'Me too!' says Pippo, grinning at Eva.

'But it will take a long time to remove these leaves.' The teacher pulls a leaf off and holds it up.

'What inside of the artichoke called?' Eva asks.

'What *is* the inside of the artichoke called,' Juliet corrects. 'It is the heart.' She looks down at the job in hand, at the artichokes that fill her sink. 'Whilst I prepare… you remember the word prepare, Eva?' Eva nods. 'So, while I prepare the artichokes, perhaps you two would like to walk around the garden together?' Juliet looks at Eva and smiles. Her action is blatant. She has guessed his reason for being here and he internally thanks her.

Eva walks into the sun with him and the cat joins them. Pippo leads her around the end of the building, where he is delighted to see the garden opens up into an area that is cared for but in an informal way, and maintains a natural look. Long grass has been left in some corners, and butterflies flit in abundance over the wild flowers that grow there. The centre of the lawn has been mown and it is even and flat, and by a natural-looking pond is an old, gnarled olive tree around which is a rough wooden bench. They head towards it.

'Shall we sitting?' she invites him. 'Am I still to be speaking in English, do you think?' Her eyes meet his but just for a second.

'Both English and Greek are second languages for me, so I will struggle a bit with either,' he replies in Greek.

'Have you found your relatives yet?' She looks down at her hands, resting lightly in her lap.

'No, but I have a strong feeling about this village of yours. Something is here for me. Or is that crazy?'

'Everything is crazy and nothing is crazy.'

'Ah, you are a philosopher!'

She makes a noise as if disputing this statement and then says, 'And what are you?'

He feels his cheeks colour. It's a good question, and he has no idea what to answer.

He leans over and picks a daisy from by the root of the old olive tree. With its stem between his finger and thumb, he spins the flower, the pink tips of the leaves merging with the white and then, without really thinking about it, he hands it to Eva.

'Will you stay here in the village?' he says.

'What? Where else would I go?' The question seems to choke her.

'Do you not want to see the world?'

'Oh I see. You mean for a holiday.'

'Well, maybe... I was thinking a bit more than a holiday. Travelling.'

'I have never really thought of it. I suppose I had just assumed that I will get married and have children because that is what I see here in the village. But now you mention it,' she looks up from her lap and beyond the limits of the garden, 'I think I would like that.' Her voice is animated.

They sit in silence for a while, not sure what to say. Then he picks up a bug and shows it to her, and her initial reaction is to exclaim 'Ew!' and back away.

'No, look. It won't hurt you,' he encourages. 'It cannot fly at you. Just look!' He looks closely at the beetle, noting the way its body glistens and shines in the sunlight, like oil on water, and Eva's eyes shine too and he thinks about kissing her but he is not sure to how make that move. As they peer closer, it opens its wings and buzzes away, making her jump. They both laugh.

'I thought you said it couldn't fly!'

He shrugs and she wags a finger at him but the smile on her face says he is forgiven.

They sit in silence for a while, and then she asks him about his travels, where he has been. His journey here feels very mundane to him; a coach and a boat and a bus, but she wants every detail.

And then he says quietly, 'Perhaps you would like the adventure of going with me when I leave?' It feels like a daring thing to say, and he wonders if he could be more daring still and kiss her. Their heads are closer together now. He lifts his chin and looks into her eyes.

The smell of artichokes starts to infuse the air, even out here in the garden. It seems to have taken no time at all for Juliet to prepare the food.

'You must be hungry, you two. Come and have some stew,' she calls, coming around the corner. Eva looks at her watch as they walk to the house.

'Do you need to be somewhere else?' Pippo asks.

'My brothers look out for me. They like to know where I am.'

'Your brothers are controlling.'

Her sudden stare is hard.

'If you did not know they had your best interests in mind, of course.' Pippo tries amend his comment.

'No, you are right. They are controlling. No one ever says that, though. They say they are protective and concerned, so I feel I have no right to complain.'

On the terrace at the front of the house, Juliet has laid the table with bread and olives and a big green salad.

'I hope you found it interesting to speak English with someone new?' Juliet asks Eva in Greek.

Before Eva can speak, Pippo says, 'It is always good to talk to someone new in any language.'

The bread is torn off in chunks, the olives are passed, and Juliet ladles stew into their bowls and pours them all water from a jug half full of ice, but as time passes, Eva becomes more agitated.

'I really must go,' she says and puts her spoon down, her bowl still half full of stew.

'Really?' Juliet asks, her eyebrows rising. 'Your family knows you are here. They will not be worried, will they?'

The stew is amazing, and Pippo is reluctant to leave it, but he puts down his own spoon.

'I will walk you,' he offers.

'I will just help Kyria Juliet…' Eva stands and begins to clear the table.

'No, it's fine Eva. Leave everything. I want a leisurely lunch,' Juliet says. 'You two go.'

Pippo closes the gate behind him and walks close to Eva down the narrow lane, so close that their hands occasionally touch, their fingers brushing. When they are nearly at the end of the lane, he has mustered enough courage to take her hand, but after the briefest of seconds, Eva slips hers free.

'He might be around.'

'Your baba?'

'No, Nikos. My elder brother.'

This must be the brother who was in the kitchen at Eva's house. He is not as tall or as broad as his baba, but there is a menace about him, as if he is permanently angry. Pippo has never thought of himself as a coward, but he would not like to get into a fight with Nikos.

Sure enough, as they join the road that leads to the village square, he is there, loitering by the taps where the old women fill their water bottles. He is with three friends who all look up, as if they have been waiting. By the side of the road, leaning on their stands, are three motorcycles.

Another bike comes buzzing up the road from the square and the rider pulls a wheelie as he passes the group. The boys cheer and the one on the bike lands the front wheel with a bump, brakes, puts his foot on the ground and leans, making the back wheel spin him round to face the opposite way for another pass. Pippo watches the bike but as it passes, Eva's face comes into his line of vision. It is blanched white, and she is staring at the group of boys. Her brother, Nikos, is also ignoring the daredevil, staring back at her. He pushes himself away from the wall he is leaning on, folds his arms, and says in a loud voice, 'What have we here?'

The rest of the boys turn their attention to Pippo now. The sun is high in the sky, but not directly above them, and it's in his eyes, making it hard to read the expressions on their faces. Certainly the mood is not friendly.

'Who's this then?' one of the boys asks.

'An Italian,' Eva's brother says and spits on the ground.

'Same face, same race,' Pippo quotes to them.

'What did he say? I can't understand his accent. Did you say you want to race?' The boy on the bike seizes the opportunity.

'No chance. He doesn't look like he's ever ridden a bike in his life,' Nikos replies.

'Not sure I would want a sister of mine with a man who can't ride a motorbike,' the thin youth next to Eva's brother pipes up.

'That's a good point, Petro!' the brother replies.

'Come on, let's go,' Eva says to Pippo and starts down the road towards the square.

The boy on the bike, who has stopped his wheelies and is now with the others, revs his engine, spins the back wheel round, and stops the bike directly in front of them, barring the way. Pippo feels his heart rate increase. His instinct is to run but that is not who he wants to be, and in any case, Eva is watching.

'I think you should take that as a challenge,' the boy on the bike says and revs the engine once more, performs another wheelie all the way to the edge of the village square. When he stops and the front wheel comes down, the boy struggles for control, the tires screech, and he puts a foot on the ground. Just when it looks like he is certain to fall, he brings the bike back under his command and spins it around, facing the group of boys. His gang mutter 'yeah,' 'well done,' and 'nice one'. Further down the road there are potholes, and the condition of the road is not good.

'Can you do that?' The boy on the bike comes back to them slowly, playing it cool by using his legs to push his bike along.

'Ignore them.' Eva pulls at Pippo's T-shirt, but he doesn't move. He leans closer to her and whispers, 'If I do this, they might leave me alone.' He feels her breath briefly on his cheek but he does not give her a chance to reply. He strides over to the bike and grabs the handlebars. The boy looks nervously over to Nikos who nods, and he surrenders the bike to Pippo, who swings his leg over as if he spends every day riding a bike. 'A wheelie to the town square then?' he says.

'All the way to the crossroads,' Nikos says.

The group start to mutter. Pippo picks up the word 'police,' 'pushing it,' 'not a good idea,' and 'potholes.' Eva's eyes are on him.

'Niko, stop it! He cannot see who is coming at the crossroad. It's dangerous!' Eva implores her brother.

He shrugs.

'Only do it if you have the guts,' he says to Pippo, arms folded across his chest, leaning back against the wall again.

Pippo revs the bike, getting the feel of its engine, breathing heavily and clenching his jaw. He revs again and kicks it into gear, letting out the clutch and taking off at great speed. He leans back and twists on the grip to rev the engine, gets the front wheel off the road, feeling the unfamiliar bike, concentrating on his balance. He's in control, the bike is light, well balanced. It's almost easy. But up ahead is the patch with the potholes, and he's going fast. Too fast to stop. No chance to swerve and the wheel hits the pothole, the bike jumps in the air, going fast, lands awkwardly, and he does not have the control he wants.

All senses alert, the crossroads loom suddenly closer than he expected. He can hear a yell from the boys behind him. But above their baritone voices, a high pitched 'No!' from Eva. The bike swerves, tyres struggle to grip the tarmac. The rear wheel slides, then holds. Pippo leans, regains control, brakes hard to slow himself. It will be alright; he can stop just in time. Sweat trickles into his eyes.

And just then, from nowhere, a cat makes a dive across the road and Pippo swerves again, the back end of the bike hits another pothole and this time there's no saving it and he lands with a thud, sliding on the rough tarmac. At least he had slowed down and there will be no serious damage, either to him or to the bike.

He flicks his hair back and looks towards the boys, jumps up as if to show that the fall was of no consequence, but his elbow is skinned and bleeding and throbs painfully. Eva is running towards him and the boys follow but then, as if they are one, they halt suddenly and look past Pippo and the bike. Pippo looks round too, to see a policeman stepping out of the corner shop. The policeman takes in the scene, scanning the road, the fallen bike, and Pippo, whose shoulders slump, and he brushes the dust off his jeans and inspects the graze on his elbow.

Agginares – Artichoke Stew

This is a warming, wholesome stew – great for cold winter evenings … Best made with fresh artichokes if you can get them, although they can be a pain to prepare!

Ingredients

4-5 spring onions, chopped (including the green bits)

2 shallots, quartered

2 big carrots, cut into slices

10-12 salad potatoes, cut into halves (you can also use big potatoes and just cut them into bite-sized chunks)

10 artichoke hearts, halved (You can use canned ones but fresh are better if you can get them)

Juice of 1 juicy lemon

About 3 cups / 750ml of water or vegetable broth

1 tablespoon plain flour

3+3 tablespoons olive oil

2 tablespoons fresh dill, chopped (or dried)

Handful of fresh parsley

Salt and pepper to taste

Directions

In a large pot, heat 3 tablespoons olive oil on a lower medium heat. Add the spring onions and shallots and let them cook for a few minutes until soft.

Add the carrots and potatoes and let them roast for about 2 or 3 minutes.

Add the tablespoon of flour (it is a binding agent and makes the stew a bit thicker), and give it another stir.

Add the water/vegetable broth, the lemon juice, the other 3 tablespoons of olive oil and some salt.

Turn up the heat and bring to a boil. Then turn down the heat a little again and let it simmer for about 10 minutes until your potatoes and carrots are soft.

Add the artichoke hearts, the dill, and some more salt and pepper to your liking.

Let it simmer for another 3 minutes until the artichoke hearts are heated up and the aromas have combined. If you are using fresh artichokes you'll need to add them earlier so they can cook.

Turn off the heat, add some freshly chopped parsley, give it another good swirl and taste your stew before serving. Add more lemon juice to taste. Serve steaming hot with fresh crusty bread and feta. Enjoy!

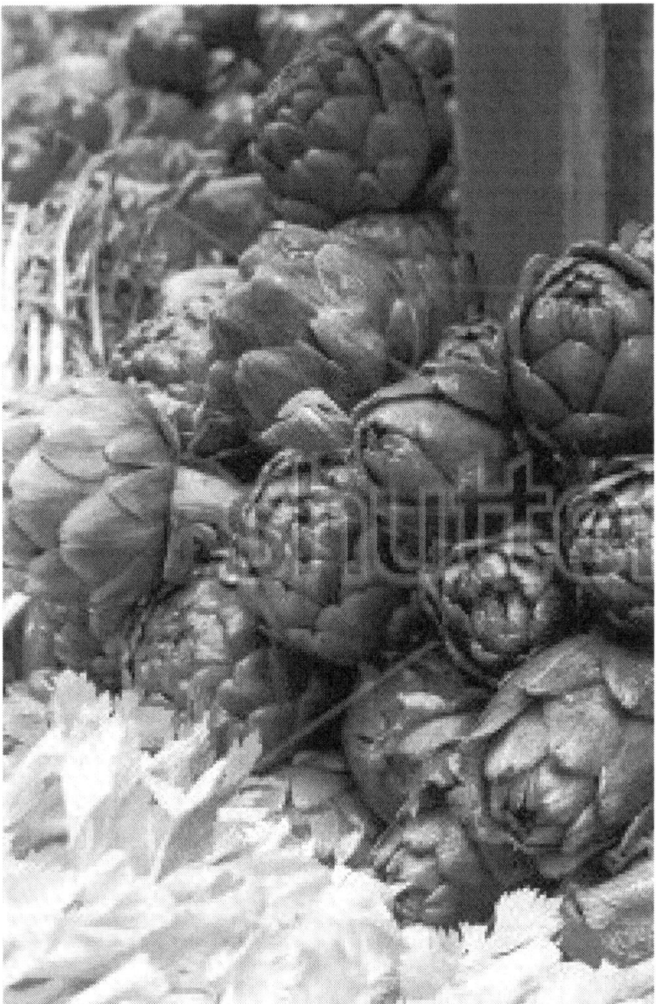

Chapter 9

'So you had to arrest him?' The woman seems to take up most of the space in the office, hands on her hips, her voice echoing around the sterile room. The tiles on the floor are cracked and there are pieces missing, the walls grubby, especially behind the policeman's chair. A fly buzzes in and out of the open window, and a thin grey ribbon rises from the overflowing ashtray on the desk, billowing and dispersing. The policeman sits behind the desk, laboriously filling out forms, surrounded by papers and coffee cups, and ignores the woman. Pippo is opposite him, inspecting his forearm, which has now stopped bleeding and is beginning to form a scab. The only other person in the room is another policeman who is going through a filing cabinet in the corner.

'It seems a bit extreme. How old are you?' she asks Pippo.

'Katerina, will you please not get involved in police business? I've had a warning already this month.' The policeman sighs. 'Why are you even here anyway?'

'I have no problem at all staying out of your business as long as your business is sensible. But when I see you arresting small children, you expect me to stand by? Do we not have a child his age at home, Michali?'

'Well, he is not our child.' Michalis puts down his pen and looks up at her, sighing again. 'What did you want anyway?'

'How old are you, boy?' Katerina's voice is kind and soft, as if he is a young child.

'Katerina, please,' the policeman implores.

'Eighteen. Well, I will be in about a month.' Pippo smiles at the woman's manner, and equally enjoys the look on her husband's face as a result of the way she disagrees with him. It gives him a sense of power.

'There, see? He is only a child. And you are suggesting what? That you throw him in with all those criminals? All those foreigners! Frighten the life out of the poor boy at best, and at worst he might find out some of the real criminals' evil ways.' She crosses herself three times.

'Katerina, these boys in the village have been warned. We have had complaints. My sergeant said the next time, I must set an example.'

'And your example is to throw a seventeen-year-old boy in with hardened criminals?'

'And what do you suggest I do? I cannot let the boy go back to the village tonight. The other boys, the ones egging him on and that were left behind, have to know that there are consequences. We make an example of this one and it sends a message to them all!'

'Then he can stay in our guest room.'

'Katerina, please! This is police business.'

'I will not have it! He is not going to jail. He is too young.' She stands behind Pippo's chair and her hands rest on his shoulders protectively. He stops picking at his scab and sits a little taller but avoids the policeman's eye.

'I have no choice.' The policeman's shoulders drop. He admits defeat. Pippo almost feels sorry for him. He is only doing his job after all, and it's clear the woman is not going to give up. The other policeman leaves the room, walking slowly down the corridor. Pippo watches him. He is a tall man, but slight. When he gets to the far end, he pushes a bar and sunlight floods the corridor and outlines the man. His head almost touches the top of the doorframe as he cups his hands, lights up, and breathes in deeply, letting out a cloud of smoke. The argument in the room continues.

'For goodness sake, have you no intelligence? If you really must do this, then just put him in your office on the daybed! But you are not putting him in with those criminals!' She tightens her grip on his shoulders. 'I could not bear the thought of our boy in there with them. You think I could face this boy's mama if we did that to him?'

Pippo grimaces, hoping they will not ask where his parents are, where he is staying. Does he say Mitsos's place? What will Mitsos think if he knows he is at the police station?

'Katerina, you're going to get me the sack,' Michalis grumbles.

'Well, I came to ask you what you would like me to bring in for your supper, but I'll not ask now. You will get what you get and there will be enough for the boy.' She releases her grip and pats his shoulders now, as if he is an obedient dog. 'I will also bring in a sheet.' She smiles kindly at Pippo and he gives her the sweetest look in return. 'Just a child,' she says as she leaves, down the corridor where the policeman stubs out his cigarette underfoot and returns indoors.

'It's alright. She's gone,' Michalis says and sighs deeply, puts his feet up on the desk, crossed at the ankles. Pippo sits patiently, waiting to see what will unfold next, both amused and fascinated by the scene that is playing out. Right from when Eva's brother challenged him, it has been something of an adventure and not the frightening experience he would have expected such a series of events to be. There is something so human about the policemen that makes him feel strangely safe. Also, even as he was being put in the back of the police car, he could sense the events working in his favour; there was a tear in Eva's eye and, even better, the look of horror and awe on her brother's face. He will be worried now, no doubt, that he is laying the blame on him.

'So, shall I bang this young man up then?' the tall police man asks.

'I wish it was so simple. Katerina will be back with the food later…'

The tall policeman shakes his head and smiles, shrugging.

'What is she making for us to eat tonight?'

It seems Katerina visits daily and the policemen have chosen to eat well and have a quiet life. Pippo leans back in his chair, crosses his arms over his chest, and crosses his ankles. This is probably going to be a long evening and maybe an even longer night, depending on whether it is the policemen or Katerina who gets their way. He looks around him, at the grey room with its light grey linoleum. The daybed against the wall looks unused. The thin mattress does not sag and the pillow is plump and untouched. If Katerina brings a cover, he will be quite comfortable here, if the policemen allow it. He wonders if he should let Mitsos know where he is, but there is no way to contact him.

'So, should I log him or not?' Michalis asks the tall policeman as another uniformed man enters the room, briefly looks at Pippo, and then pulls a chair away from the wall to sit with his colleagues.

'What's Katerina cooking today?' he asks, but the others ignore him.

'If you log him, you will have to put him in a cell with the others.'

'If I do not log him, then we are holding him illegally,' Michalis says. The new policeman looks from the one to the other and then at Pippo.

'So you may as well let him go,' the tall policeman says and he finds his own chair and sits lightly on the edge, leaning forward, his elbows on his knees.

'If I let him ago, there will be no discipline in that village and the sergeant might get to hear that we let the opportunity pass us by.'

'Stalemate,' Pippo says.

'What?' Michalis sounds shocked that he has spoken.

'You cannot win.'

No one speaks.

'But I think I can help you out. That day bed looks comfortable enough and a cup of coffee in the morning would be nice?' Pippo smiles his best smile.

A night on the day bed in the office will be no hardship. In his mind's eye, Pippo recalls the look of concern on Eva's face as he was taken away, and the shock and horror on the brother's face. If he spends a night away from the village, that horror will sink deeply into the brother's mind and, equally, Eva might fall asleep thinking he is the hero.

'You mean you will stay voluntarily? Why?' Michalis asks suspiciously.

Pippo weighs up how best to answer. He wants to avoid having to answer any questions about where he is staying or where home is, or if they need to contact anyone. So far, he has been lucky that they have not asked him any of those questions yet. So right now he needs to steer them away from that line of thought.

'I am happy to stay voluntarily because if I don't tell on the other boys, they might stop bullying me and also,' he gives a conspiratorial wink to them all, 'I might get the girl.'

All three policemen seem to find this funny and, best of all, they seem satisfied that he is being honest. The tall, thin one lets out a deep belly laugh that sounds as if it should come from someone much rounder.

'So you are going to stay here for a woman?' Michalis laughs. 'Be careful what you wish for!'

'I'll not hear a word against Katerina. At least she's a good cook,' the tall one says.

The new policeman takes a pack of cards from his pocket, the atmosphere in the room now relaxed.

'Well, if we are here for the evening, then let's enjoy ourselves.'

Within minutes, the official papers have been cleared away, coffee cups balanced on the windowsill, and a lively game of cards begins. At first, they stake matchsticks, but soon the new policeman wants to bet real money and they subsidise Pippo. Within ten minutes, he wins his subsidy back and half an hour later, he is winning all the money.

'I don't believe it!' the tall policeman says. 'Brought in for disorderly behaviour and he'll walk away a rich man.' He laughs and slaps Pippo on the back.

'Not only rich but well fed!' Michalis clears the cards away as the aroma of roasted tomatoes and herbs filters down the corridor. By the time Katerina enters with her tray, there is no evidence of the card game.

'Shelf, go get some water and cups,' Katerina demands of the tall policeman.

'Shelf? That's a funny name,' Pippo says.

'He's had that name since that day he was asked to put the shelves up.' Michalis points to a line of files on a shelf, high up on the wall. 'No one can reach them but him!'

The tall policeman returns with plastic cups of water. Katerina serves, offering a choice of stuffed tomatoes or peppers to each man, ladling them onto the plates from a large metal oven dish.

She gives Pippo one of each, and plenty of roast potatoes. The three policemen begin to eat with relish and no one speaks.

'Don't let it get cold,' Katerina says to Pippo and throws a quilt she has brought onto the daybed. She winks at him as she leaves, and glares at Michalis.

'Oh my stripes!' the new policeman says. 'Your wife has outdone herself! Sultanas in the rice, in the tomatoes, and pinenuts in with the peppers.'

'It smells amazing.' Pippo lifts his fork. He is in for a good evening of eating, more cards no doubt, and a good night's sleep.

Gemista – Stuffed Tomatoes

Gemista (stuffed tomatoes) is such a quintessentially Greek dish, and it's super easy to make and very satisfying.

Essentially it's a risotto made using the juice of the tomatoes, that is then baked inside the tomato shells with roast potatoes…

Serve with crusty bread, feta and a nice glass of wine. Yum!!

As with all the recipes in this book there are many variations. I use lots of mint, and always add pine nuts and raisins or sultanas, but you can experiment with other herbs such as parsley and dill, for example.

Ingredients

8 big tomatoes

4 green bell peppers

5-6 potatoes, cut into wedges

2 red onions, finely chopped

2 cloves of garlic, finely chopped. More if you want.

500g/ 18 oz / 2.5 cups rice (for risotto)

A large bunch of fresh mint, chopped

Salt and freshly ground pepper

Olive oil

A handful of pine nuts

A handful of raisins/sultanas

Directions

Wash the tomatoes and the peppers, slice the lids off, and scoop out the insides of the tomatoes with a spoon. Try not to make holes in the skins of the tomatoes. Scoop the seeds out of the peppers and discard.

Blend the insides of the tomatoes (the flesh and the juice that you scooped out) and set aside for later.

In a large frying pan, sauté the onions and garlic in olive oil. Add the tomato juice that you blended along with the pine nuts, raisins, mint and salt and pepper and bring to the boil. Turn down to a low heat and add the rice, and simmer till it is nearly cooked. It's ok if the rice still has a bit of a bite because in the next step you will bake it in the oven. Keep stirring so the rice doesn't stick, and add water if it begins to dry out. Don't make it too wet though – you want to end up with the liquid absorbed by the rice.

In a large baking tray assemble the gemista. Spoon the filling into the empty vegetables and place the potatoes, cut into pieces, in between the vegetables. Season with salt and pepper and drizzle over olive oil Put the lids back on the tomatoes and peppers.

Bake at 350 Fahrenheit / Gas 4 / 180 degrees for 60-75 minutes. Cover with foil if necessary to stop the vegetables drying out.

Serve warm with crusty bread and feta. Like many Greek dishes, gemista can be even better the next day!

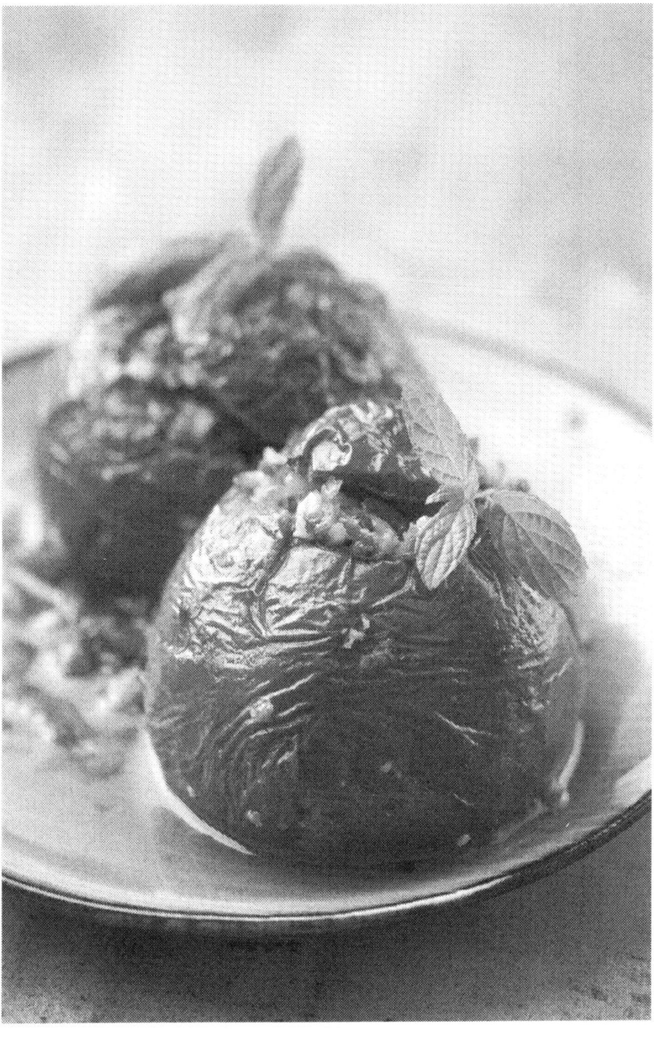

Chapter 10

Pippo is roused from a deep sleep early the next morning by the patter of feet down the corridor and a tuneless humming. Katerina strolls into the room and dumps a cluster of keys with police tags hanging from the fob on the desk. Next to this she places a bag from which she takes fresh bread, local butter, she tells him, and a jar of quince jam that she bought recently at a sale to raise money to neuter the local cats. He tries to appear interested as he yawns and stretches, shaking off the sleep.

With a smile, Katerina takes a small, single-burner portable gas stove from the cupboard in the desk along with the tiniest pan he has ever seen. Out come other items: a small cup, a bag of sugar, a spoon, a packet of coffee, a bottle of water. Within minutes, the aroma of Greek coffee fills the room. The taste is even better than the espresso he is used to. Pippo sips at the hot, sweet coffee and the outer door clangs open for the second time.

Michalis strides purposefully into the room, marches to the table, and picks up the keys, stuffs them in his own pocket, and clatters about with the drawers, extracts a pile of papers, and drops them with a bang.

'I looked everywhere for my keys!' he grumbles. 'It was only when I saw your shoes gone and the gate open that I put two and two together!'

'Oh, don't fuss,' Katerina dismisses him but Michalis is serious and he pulls her by the arm into the corridor. Through the half-closed door, Pippo can hear him barking at his wife.

'Never do this again!' He is trying his very best to sound menacing but he is a gentle man by nature and

Pippo suspects that this expression of his anger will only endear him to Katerina. Through the crack in the door, he sees her plant a kiss on Michalis's cheek and then she turns and leaves without another word. Michalis tuts and clicks his tongue as re-enters the room, shaking his head slowly. Pippo pretends he has not seen and busies himself with folding the cover Michalis's wife so kindly provided him with.

'Okay, so my sergeant will be here in an hour,' the policeman says. 'I will take you back to the village after that.' He sits heavily and rubs his forehead, gazing blankly out the window.

'That was a good night,' Pippo ventures. After the food, they had resumed playing cards. Then the night shift had come, but Michalis and his party remained, a bottle of ouzo appeared, and they began to bet on each game for bigger and bigger stakes with Pippo still winning more often than not. By the time the day shift left, Michalis had had to be supported by the other two as they stumbled down the corridor.

'We could get a bottle on the way home?' he said, waving goodnight to Pippo over his shoulder.

'I think you've had enough,' the tall one called Shelf answered.

The sergeant appears after an hour or so and praises Michalis for helping send a message to the youth of the village about menacing the other residents.

The ride back to the village is taken steadily with Michalis frequently rubbing his forehead. He pulls up against the curb just outside the village.

'Okay, well, mind how you go,' he says to Pippo.

Pippo wonders how much of last night the policeman remembers.

'Sure,' he replies jovially as he climbs out of the police car. 'And thanks to your wife for her wonderful cooking.'

Pushing his hands deep into his front pockets, he sets off with a little whistle on his lips towards the village square. The police car turns around behind him and returns the way it came. The policeman did not once ask where he was from, where he was staying, or even for his full name.

'Amazing!' Pippo tells himself and there is a bounce to his step as he re-enters the village.

First he must explain to Mitsos where he was last night and then, at some point in the day, he will find Eva and her brother Nikos. His stomach twists a little at the thought and he is not sure if this is nerves or excitement. Nikos is bound to think he has put the blame on him! He may even be expecting a visit from the police himself!

Even from a distance, he can see the newspapers strung under the roof of the kiosk, showing that Vasso is already up. The eatery is still all closed up. He is a little surprised until the church clock chimes out that it is only nine o clock in the morning. Far too early for anyone wanting to eat.

Opposite the eatery is a very small shop, just a narrow window and a door. The window is open and on the sill is balanced a wooden baker's tray displaying chocolate-filled croissants, *spankopites*, *tiropites*, and twists of pastry that are flecked with orange, suggesting they might be cheesy. The smell is enticing, but it turns out it is coming from the bakery next door. A group of women with baskets stand inside and a man, not that much older than himself at a guess, is quickly taking loaves from the shelves behind him, wrapping each in paper, and passing them to the women who drop coins into the palm of his hand. In his window are wooden boxes of biscuits and it is these Pippo can smell. Maybe he could buy some with his winnings and take them to Eva's mama to thank her for her kindness yesterday. Another action that would make it difficult for Nikos to remain hostile.

'Ha!' This sound of joy escapes him and he gives a little skip. It would be a great excuse to see Eva.

Somewhere in the village, a cockerel announces the day, which sets a dog off barking, which in turn sets another one howling. The sun is already warm, the sky is cloudless; in every respect it promises to be a good day!

'Hi there. What can I get you?' The man behind the counter says to Pippo when his turn comes.

'Biscuits, a bagful.'

'What kind?' The man looks at his display in the window.

'No idea. They are for someone else.'

'Would I know them?'

'You might... Aleko's wife, from the garage.'

'Oh! Are you are going to the party? Would you take the cake along?'

Pippo thinks quickly. Better and better! How can Eva and her mama not approve of the person who delivers their cake! And how annoyed Nikos might be with that!

'Sure. I would love to. I'm Pippo, by the way.' He wonders what they are celebrating. A birthday perhaps?

'Ah, so you're Pippo. I am Fillipos. Mitsos told me your plan and I am making *ravani* for Stella's table.' He grins as if nothing would give him greater pleasure.

'What's that?'

'*Ravani*? It's a traditional Greek cake, one of the *siropiasta*, which, basically, means a syrupy dessert. Wait till you taste it. Do you like coconut?'

'Yes, I suppose so. I don't dislike it.'

'Ah, you will love this. The trick is when adding syrup to the cake, always make sure that the cake is cold and the syrup is really hot. So you ladle it on really slowly so each spoonful is really absorbed.' He mimes how he would do this, lifting an invisible ladle high in the air. 'You pour it over evenly, and don't forget the edges. Then, of course, most people cut it up and eat it, but if you can, you want to wait until it is cool so it doesn't crumble. Pretty irresistible!' He smacks his lips. Pippo checks Fillipos's waistline. For someone who obviously enjoys what he makes, he is very trim.

'That sounds amazing!'

'It is! Now, what was I getting you?'

A woman comes in and waits behind Pippo.

'Oh yes, the cake. And do you still want the biscuits?'

'Sure.'

It takes but a second to fill a white paper bag with dry-looking sweet biscuits that Fillipos assures Pippo are Aleko's family's favourites, perfect for dipping in coffee. They cost him only a few cents—barely a dent in his winnings. The cake is boxed and, gripping the bag of biscuits in his fist, he rests the box on his arm and holds it steady with the other hand.

'See you at Stella's!' Fillipos calls after him.

'Yes, see you there.' Pippo looks over his shoulder back at the baker as he leaves. If he is to stay in this village any length of time, maybe he will go for a beer with Fillipos, who seems like he might be good company.

'What have you got there?' Aleko straightens up from under the bonnet of a car as Pippo arrives. He wipes his forehead with the back of his hand, leaving a smear of oil.

'Delivery.'

'Oh yes!' Aleko glances at the house, as if the cake is a secret but then says, 'Can you take it inside?'

'Sure.'

Aleko bends under the bonnet again as Pippo makes his way around the side of the house. The table where Eva was baking is now laden with plates and cutlery. There is a tube of plastic cups and a jug of water with cling film over the top. Maybe he should leave the bag of biscuits on the table to be discovered later. Or maybe …

'Ah, Pippo, what have you there?' Eva's mama steps out into the sunshine, a smudge of flour across her forehead. Pippo grins.

'The cake, and I brought you some biscuits too.' He offers them both up to her.

'Oh, bring them in. Can you?' She shows him her hands that are covered in flour. 'I am in the middle of everything.'

The kitchen is in mayhem. Every available surface is covered with bowls, pans, and chopping boards.

'So I just made a spinach and feta pie. Also, I have been… oh hang on, what time is it?' She looks at her watch. 'Oh it's over ten hours now, so they must be ready. Do you like *gigantes*?'

'Giants?' Pippo asks, listening for noises in the rest of the house, trying to work out who else is around. It is very quiet.

'Well, look.' She tips a bowl towards him. 'Are they not big, giants of the bean world perhaps? And they are really fat now they have been soaking for ten hours. Actually, I have left it a little late to get started, as I usually cook them for two hours. But I guess I can put the temperature up and maybe they'll be good in an hour. The sauce is so simple. Oh, sorry! I have left you holding the cake.' She clears a space on the table and he is just setting down the box carefully when Eva comes in the room. His heart misses a beat and then races to catch up with itself.

'You brought the cake?' she asks quietly, her eyes on his, her pupils dilated as if with fear, and it takes him a moment to remember that the last time she saw him, he was being taken away in a police car. It is as if seeing him again has taken her back to that moment. In the corridor behind her, someone moves in the shadows. Nikos steps into the light in the kitchen and looks from Pippo to his mama twice in rapid succession. He seems nervous, scared perhaps that Pippo has told his mama what happened. Pippo wonders if he can use this to his advantage, tease Nikos a little, but he cannot think how, so he smiles and both Eva and Nikos's faces relax just a little.

'Eva, I am going to boil the beans up now. Can you watch them?' Eva's mama asks. 'Don't get distracted and forget about them, and make sure you scoop off the froth or it will go all over the stove.' She turns to Nikos. 'Meanwhile, could you two go and get some lemons?' Eva looks at Pippo, and now she seems nervous.

Nikos leads the way down the corridor and they go outside, past the table and into the backyard. Pippo's heart beats just a little quicker as he tries to gauge what Niko's mood might be towards him.

'There is a lemon tree at the back here.' He walks past the table and Pippo catches a glimpse of Eva looking through the kitchen window at him, a spoon in her hand. The lemon tree is amongst some orange trees near the back wall. Nikos gives the appearance of being in a hurry and all the bravado he has shown previously seems to have evaporated. In fact, when he is around his family, he seems to be the opposite of who he shows himself to be with his friends. He is polite, courteous, and even a little shy. Once they are in amongst the leaves, Nikos stops and turns on him.

'So what did you say? What happened?' The lemons are forgotten.

'Ah, well,' Pippo says slowly. Nikos closes the space between them. His brow lowers. It is not Nikos's size that is intimidating; it is the impression that he could do something unexpected and not care. But then, Pippo reasons with himself, he cared enough to be concerned that something had been said to his mama. Maybe it is all show.

'What would you have done? Blamed it on someone else to save your skin?' Pippo stands his ground.

'No.' The answer is quick but it does not sound so sure. 'Is that what you did?'

'I spent the night in the police station.'

'Really?' Nikos does not manage to quite close his mouth after he has spoken. He just stares.

'Yes, really, and it was a very thin mattress.'

'Oh my God. They put you in a cell!'

'There were three in the room.' Technically it is not a lie. 'Men, big men, not boys.'

Nikos has blanched white.

'The food was not too bad. In fact, pretty good.'

'Did they, you know, push you around?'

'Well, they all tried.' Pippo thinks of the card game. 'They saw me as a young rookie, but I showed them a thing or two.'

'Ah, you're lying!' Nikos's laugh is brittle and his eyes flash. He is testing.

'Take a look at this then.' Pippo scoops out the notes from his pockets. 'Went in with nothing, played cards with them, and won it all!'

'*Panagia mou*!' Nikos exclaims. Pippo stuffs the money back into his pockets. 'So, come on. What did you tell the police?' he says.

'Nothing.' Pippo stares hard back at him. 'I could have done, and it might have spared me the night if I had, but I didn't.'

'Thanks.' Nikos's brow unfurrows and his cheeks seem to melt.

'So I thought I would spend the money on taking Eva for a coffee and cake. It seems only fair.' He makes it sound like a statement rather than a request.

'Yes, sounds fair to me too,' Nikos says.

'Give us a leg up. I'll get some of those massive lemons up there.' Pippo takes hold of Nikos's shoulder and Nikos links his hand to make a stirrup.

Gigantes

Remember that gigantes (or large lima) beans foam up quite a bit when you cook them. Don't worry if it's your first time and don't go too far from the stove as you'll need to skim off the foam every 10-15 minutes or so. It's a messy affair should it boil over onto your stovetop.....

To boil the beans, cover with about 2-3 inches of water, do NOT add salt, and cook over medium-high heat for about 50 minutes from the time you put the pot on the heat. They should be done but not too done and will finish their cooking later in the oven.

Save two cups of the cooking water before you drain the beans. You'll need it later for the sauce; the starch from boiling the beans gives you a thicker/creamier sauce.

When ready to bake your gigantes, gently spread the boiled beans in an even layer in your pan. I find a 9x13x2 inch baking pan is perfect for 1 pound of beans (dried). For doubling or tripling the recipe, I use a large, deep ceramic casserole dish. The sides are about 4 inches high to accommodate the additional sauce.

When making the sauce, a cup of olive oil may seem overly generous but you want your finished baked beans to be creamy and this is the only fat in this dish, so pour on!

Sauté the chopped onions and celery, until they're soft, add the garlic for a minute or two until tender and then add herbs and spices. Give the pan a good stir to mix everything together evenly. Then cook for only another minute just to release the flavors and add the crushed tomato. Cook for 5 minutes to bring the sauce together and then add your reserved cooking water. Bring sauce up to a boil and set aside until ready to bake your beans.

When ready to bake, pour the sauce over the beans in the baking dish and carefully stir to incorporate everything. Add 1 cup of water (room temp) to the pan and cook at 350 degrees for 2 hours.

I give the pan a gentle stir every half hour or so but it isn't absolutely necessary if you have to leave it on its own. Most of the water will have been absorbed and it's a good idea to stir once and then allow the beans to stand undisturbed for about 15- 30 minutes before serving.

Ingredients

1 pound / 2.25 cups / 450g dried beans (gigantes or large lima beans)

2 medium onions

1/3 cup chopped garlic - 12 -14 cloves

Celery - 2-3 stalks

3/4 cup / 20g / 0.7oz chopped fresh parsley

1/3 cup / 10g / 0.3oz chopped fresh mint

1 tbsp crushed, dried oregano

1 tbsp salt

2 tsp fresh ground black pepper

1 cup / 240ml Greek olive oil

2 cups / 400g / 14.1oz crushed tomatoes

2 cups / 470ml / 8 fl oz reserved cooking water from beans

1 cup / 235ml / 4 fl oz water, room temperature

Directions

Soak dried beans overnight or at least 7 hours. Boil for 50 minutes and RESERVE 2 cups of cooking liquid before draining beans.

Sauté chopped onions and celery in olive oil over medium low heat until tender. Add garlic and cook for a few minutes until soft. Add herbs and spices, mix to combine completely and cook for just a minute to combine flavor oils.

Add chopped tomatoes, stir to combine and cook for 5 minutes. Add reserved bean cooking liquid and bring sauce up to a boil. Remove from heat and set aside until ready to bake the beans.

Layer cooked gigantes beans evenly in 9×13 baking pan and pour sauce over top. Add 1 cup room temperature water and bake, uncovered, for 2 hours in 350 degree / 180 Celsius / Gas mark 4 oven. Stir approximately every half hour or so.

Allow baked beans to rest for about 15-30 minutes before serving. Serve with crusty bread and a glass of buttery white wine for a most wonderful, traditional meal.

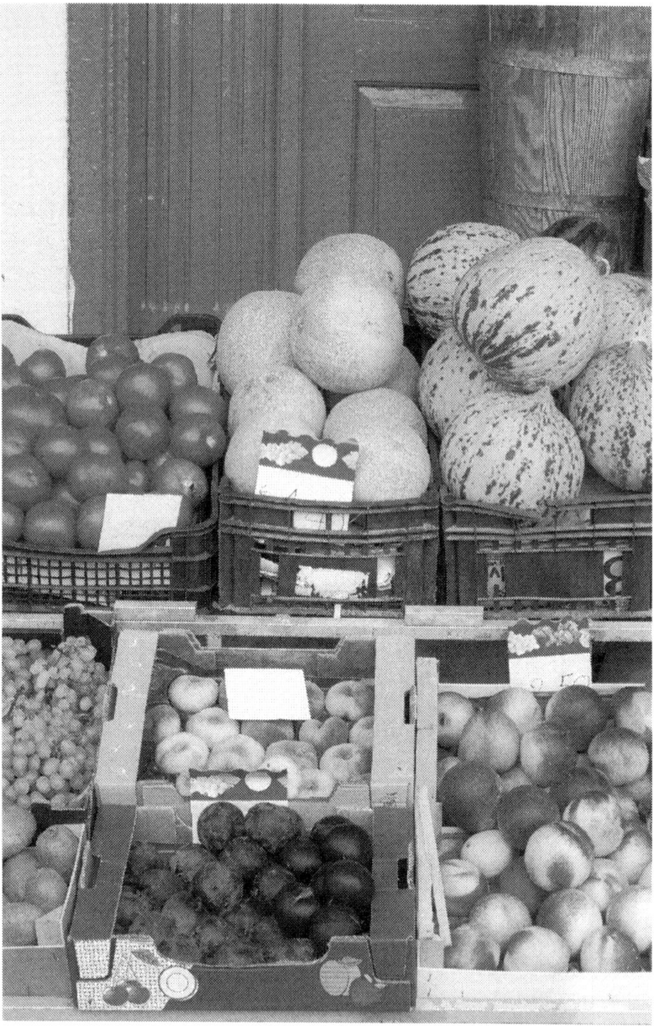

Chapter 11

It turns out it's the youngest brother's tenth birthday. Nikos points him out as they return with the lemons and refers to him as Zouki. His real name is Andreas, Eva explains later, but apparently he looked like a zucchini when he was first born and the nickname stuck. Zouki is running around the table chasing a puppy that yaps with joy, outrunning the boy easily and then pausing for him to catch up, wagging its tail so frantically that its whole body shakes. Some of Zouki's friends have arrived, uncomfortable in their best party clothes and for the most part standing awkwardly around the edge of the yard.

'Mama, we have your lemons,' Nikos calls out as they go inside and Eva appears at the kitchen door, takes one look at the two of them, exhales with relief. She smiles, thumps Nikos on the arm. Nikos leads the way through to the kitchen but Pippo grabs at Eva's hand, gently holding her back.

'I would like to take you into Saros for coffee. Will you come?' he asks and his heart leaps when she colours from her neck to the top of her forehead. She looks down at her hands, her fingers twisting on themselves.

'Tell him yes and put the poor boy out of his misery,' Eva's mama calls good-naturedly from the kitchen and Pippo colours too when he hears Nikos laughing and telling her in hushed tones to be quiet.

'Yes then!' Eva shouts back over her shoulder and meets Pippo's gaze. 'I would love to,' she says in a voice that is little more than a whisper.

'Right, so that's the *fava* done.' Athena holds a tray full of dishes which proves to be so wide that she has to turn sideways as she comes out the kitchen door and heads down the corridor and out into the yard. 'Do you like *fava*, Pippo? You will stay for the party, won't you? You can't take Eva just yet; she is needed here.' She winks at Pippo as she passes him and it makes him feel accepted, as if he is one of the family.

'I would love to stay,' he says as she steps outside, then he turns to Eva and whispers, 'What on earth is *fava*?'

'Oh, it is delicious. Usually it is a winter dish, but Zouki loves it so much. It is rich and creamy and, well, just try some. If you've never had it before, you'll be converted.' Eva speaks with a giggle in her voice. Pippo reaches for her hand, but she is quick to make a move to the kitchen.

'Can you take the *briam*?' she asks and picks up a big dish of Greek salad, a slab of feta on top that has been garnished with a slash of bright green olive oil. The oil looks like the same olive oil Mitsos used for the toasted bread dish and Pippo wonders if everyone in the village presses their own olives.

'Hey, wake up!' Eva nudges him in the ribs with her elbow. 'The *briam*?' She nods at a dish on the stove and he starts to pick it up, only to find it is hot. 'There's a cloth there.'

Hands protected with a tea towel, he lifts the roasting tray of vegetables and breathes in the scent of parsley, mint, oregano, of course, and, if he is not mistaken, basil. The dish is a mixture of potatoes, courgettes, and aubergines, with other vegetables and tomatoes, and the aroma is heady and his stomach growls in anticipation. He joins Eva and the boys outside, putting the *briam* on the table next to the salad.

'Are you hungry?' Athena calls out to the boys, who are now playing a game of football in the backyard by the orange and lemon trees. There are more of them than before.

They do not answer but instead rush over and jostle for plates and forks, serving themselves from the dishes on the table with great enthusiasm.

'Ha!' Athena says to Pippo. 'You have to be quick round here!' She gives him a nudge as she sets down a spinach pie; a spiral of *filo* pastry with cheese and spinach oozing out of the ends. 'You best get in there first with this one.' She hands him a knife.

Eva helps herself to a small portion, which she nibbles at, picking off flaky bits of pastry with neatly manicured fingers and looking into his eyes all the while.

'Do we have to stay till the end?' he whispers. Watching her eat is making him want to be alone with her.

'What on earth?' She looks past him, over his shoulder. Her wide eyes make him turn quickly. Zouki is shouting. Athena comes running out of the house flapping a tea towel. A donkey has made its way into the yard and is helping itself to whatever is left of the party food. Pippo's response is to laugh, but he tries to stifle it, aware that it will not be funny for those who have spent all morning cooking.

'The cake's not on the table, is it?' Eva thrusts her plate into his hands and runs at the animal, shooing it away. But the beast shows no fear and even seems to fancy a bite out of Athena's tea towel. Eva slaps and shoves the animal's rump but it has its eyes firmly on the remains of the green salad.

'Bloody beast!' Nikos comes flying out of the house. There's a rage in his eyes and suddenly the whole episode is no longer amusing. Pippo fears for the animal's safety. He is nimbler on his feet than Nikos and has hold of the animal by its forelock, shielding it with his body before Nikos can let his rage erupt on the defenceless animal.

'That's one of Thanasis's mangy beasts,' Nikos says, jabbing his finger in the animal's face. Eva puts a protective hand on the donkey's forehead and strokes its nose with the other. Nikos steps back a pace and Pippo and Eva exchange a look, understanding.

'So, where does this Thanasis live?' Pippo asks, leading the donkey gently away from the table and from Nikos.

'Oh, are you going to take him back? You are good,' Athena says. Nikos bristles.

'Over in some dump that way.' He half-indicates the direction with a twist of his neck and a roll of his eyes.

'I'll show you,' Eva says and they lead the animal out of the yard. Once they are on the lane and a distance from the house, Eva says, 'He can be so…' She struggles to find the right word. 'Overbearing,' she says finally.

'And you have a good heart,' he answers.

The donkey seems more than happy to be led, but every now and then it pulls its head free and bends to eat a mouthful of grass here, a clump of weeds there, from the side of the road. Once his mouth is full, he responds again to the tug on his mane.

Pippo does not feel he has to talk to Eva every second, and Eva seems to be comfortable in silence. He does, however, take her hand, and their fingers intertwine, both happy to let the donkey dictate the speed. The lane winds out of the village centre and the houses give way to orange orchards and birdsong takes over from the shouting of children and barking of dogs. The cicadas provide a continuous accompaniment.

'Have you found your family yet?' Eva asks finally.

Pippo is about to say no but he looks over at her, noting the curve of her mouth, the way her hair falls across her shoulders. 'I think I have found my family,' he says, but the moment the words are out, he knows he has said too much and his mind races to work out how he can make it sound like a joke, or at least soften the pressure of such a statement. But whilst his mind works on this, his heart is in shock that he really feels what he said is true.

'Is that possible?' His heart speaks before his mind has assessed the situation. 'I mean, people would say I am too young, that we are too young!'

'I think people would say we are lucky.' Eva speaks so quietly, he has to lean towards her to hear clearly. 'Not everyone gets a chance of happiness.' She sounds so wise. 'Look at Thanasis. He is, well I'm not sure, nearly eighty, I think. Never met anyone all his life and now suddenly he is courting Poppy, who has a sort of bric-a-brac shop over on the other side of the village. I expect, given the choice, he would rather have been our age when he met her!'

'And Mitsos, from what he has told me, has only been married three years.' Pippo squeezes her hand and looks at her mouth, wondering how she would respond if he tried to kiss her.

'That's Thanasis's place, there.' Eva points. The moment is lost.

'That place? It looks derelict.' He takes in the whitewash peeling off the stone walls of what looks like a tumbledown barn by the side of the road. In places, it is coming away in large flakes, leaving a trail of white by the roadside.

The donkey knows it is home and frees itself from Pippo's grip, and with unexpected grace, it neatly jumps the low gate and disappears round the back of the building.

'What the!' they hear a voice exclaim. 'I thought you were in the stable.'

'I guess we have no reason to go further,' Eva says. But Pippo is curious about this man who has just started courting at eighty years of age.

'Shall we not say hello?'

Eva shrugs; Thanasis is nothing new to her, of course. Nevertheless, she unlatches the gate and calls out. 'Kyrie Thanasi?'

'Now, who is that?' a voice replies.

'It is Eva and a stranger.' She smiles at Pippo as she says this. His stomach flutters at her look.

'A stranger, eh?' A man whose skin is made of parchment rounds the end of the house and hastens to open the gate for them. He exudes an aroma of fresh straw despite his suit and clean shirt.

'Kyrie Thanasi, this is Pippo, here from Italy to find his people,' Eva says.

'Ciao!' Thanasis grins and shakes Pippo's hand heartily. 'Well, I am all dressed up and ready to take Poppy out for coffee, but I was going to have a little nip to help me along my way.' He leads the way to what Pippo expects will be the back of the house, facing the orchard, and is surprised to find that the rough track that leads from the gate opens out to a neat courtyard, off which is the front door. Either side of the door has window boxes, painted a bright blue. The doors and windows are freshly painted in the same shade.

'Oh, you have the place looking nice!' Eva comments and Pippo wonders whether there were flowers and paint and window boxes before Thanasis started courting this Poppy.

'Bit of colour, bit of a clean.' Thanasis scratches his chin and picks dead heads off a geranium.

'And the yard too!' Eva says. Pippo looks about him; the yard could not be described as tidy. There is an assortment of copper pipes stacked by the nearest tree, a couple of old doors against another. To one side, under the orange trees, an area has been fenced off, and the ground behind the fence is trampled and dusty. Two donkeys hang their heads, snoozing by a water trough over which a pair of butterflies flit and dive. It is picturesque but in a practical, lived-in way.

Thanasis goes in the front door, leaving them standing in the yard. He reappears with an ouzo bottle and three glasses.

'Er, not for me, Kyrie Thanasi,' Eva says, eyeing the bottle with distaste.

'I'll take a slug with you,' Pippo says and Thanasis's quick eyes find his, stare hard, and then flick to Eva and back. He seems to be summing up the situation and Pippo nods his head ever so slightly and grins. Thanasis fills the glasses and they click rims.

'*Yeia mas!*' he says.

'*Yeia mas*,' Pippo replies and they sip their drinks whilst Eva fusses over the donkeys.

'Here's to courting!' Thanasis says quietly. 'And talking of which, are you the young man setting up this table with Mitsos for Stella?'

'I am!' The ouzo is warming Pippo's veins, making him feel strong.

'Well, you can tell Mitsos I have thought of a dish.' Eva rejoins them. Thanasis tosses back the last of his ouzo and slams his glass down on the top of a solid wide log whose scarred surface indicates all the times it has been used to split kindling on. Pippo finishes his drink while Thanasis closes the door to the house—but does not bother to lock it, Pippo notes. He leads the way, muttering that he does not want to be late.

'So this dish,' he says once they are out on the lane. 'I am not sure it is fancy enough.'

'It doesn't have to be fancy,' Pippo says. He is walking next to Eva and he feels for her hand. She finds his and their fingers interlock once more.

'Well, if he'll have it, I'll make my aubergine and potato *stifado*. Like I said, it is not fancy, and most people put in octopus or beef, but being a bachelor all my life, vegetables is about as good as it gets in my kitchen.' Thanasis seems to find this funny.

'I love *stifado*. We have it for lunch often,' Eva says. Pippo tries to imagine how the dish Thanassis describes could be considered a main course. But then again, until recently he wouldn't have thought toast and olive oil would be so great either, so best wait until he tries it!

'So, they tell me you are courting someone called Poppy?' He enquires of Thanasis.

'Ah yes indeed, and at my age! Now if I was your age…'

'What would you do if you were my age?' Pippo looks at Eva.

'If I was your age, I would grab the opportunity with both hands and hold tight. I am not sure how many chances we get in a lifetime, and I have made a mess of a few, but this one, well, it's Poppy, isn't it!'

'You've known her long then?'

'Known her since I was your age and made the big mistake of letting her get away and losing a lifetime because of it.' Thanasis leans close to speak into Pippo's ear. 'Don't lose a second, lad,' he whispers, the smell of aniseed on his breath.

The village square is in sight.

'I might have to go on to the *kafenio* for another little bit of courage,' Thanasis says.

'I don't think it is courage you want,' Pippo replies, 'so much as a push. Where does this Poppy live?'

'Up that lane over there.'

'Then keep walking, my friend.' Pippo walks between Thanasis and the kafenio, blocking the way to the door.

'Here.' Eva passes him a handful of wildflowers she has collected from the roadside. 'For Poppy.'

'Ah, that is right nice of you,' Thanasis says.

'I think you've missed the point, Thanasis. I think Eva has given them to you to give to Poppy from yourself.' Pippo clarifies.

'Oh, yes, right.' He looks at the flowers and a flush of colour appears around his neck. 'Well, wish me luck.' They are at the far edge of the square. Eva's house is in one direction, Poppy's in another, and if Pippo is to see Mitsos today, his direction is yet another way.

'Good luck!' Pippo and Eva speak in unison as Thanasis begins to walk away.

Stifado

This vegetarian version of the classic Greek lamb casserole is made with earthy aubergines, flavoursome olives and fluffy potatoes, seasoned with cinnamon and cloves. Best served with rice or couscous.

Ingredients

300g (10oz) / 1 cup new potatoes, scrubbed and quartered

2 tbsp olive oil

1 large onion, chopped

1 aubergine, cut into 1cm (1/2 inch) slices

2 large garlic cloves, finely chopped

1 cinnamon stick

6 cloves

2 tsp dried oregano

2 tbsp red wine vinegar

1 x 500g / 2.25 cups / 17.9oz pack sieved passata

2 tbsp tomato paste

150g (5oz) / 2 cups butter beans, from a can, drained

75g (3oz) / aprox half a cup pitted black olives, from a jar, drained

Directions

Boil the potatoes in plenty of salted water for 12–14 minutes or until tender. Drain and leave until cool enough to handle, then peel off skins.

Meanwhile, heat the oil in a large casserole dish over a medium heat and cook the onion for 5 minutes, covered and stirring occasionally.

Add the aubergine and cook, covered, for another 8 minutes until tender.

Add the garlic, cinnamon, cloves and oregano and stir well.

Pour in the vinegar, passata and 200ml (7fl oz) water. Add the tomato paste, butter beans, olives and cooked potatoes and bring to the boil. Turn the heat down, part-cover with a lid, and simmer for 20 minutes, stirring regularly, until reduced and thickened.

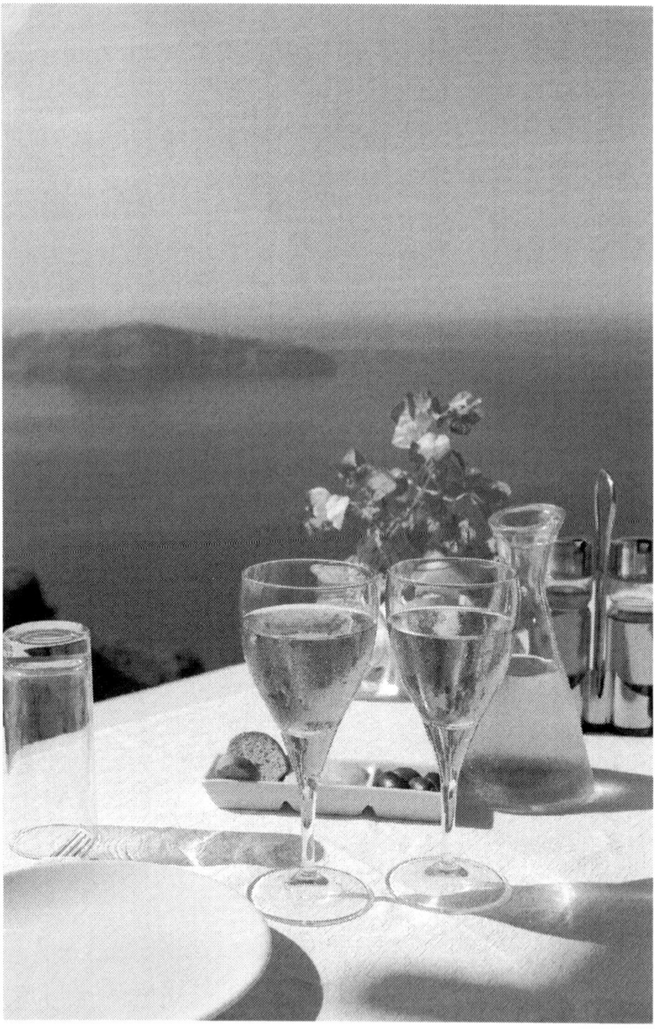

Chapter 12

'Hey, are you Pippo?' a voice calls and Pippo spins round to see a man come bouncing out of the kafenio. At first glance he seems young, but in the sunlight it becomes clear that he has seen some years. His mop of hair, a halo of grey, appears to defy gravity and by his eyes are deep smile lines, as if he has spent all his years laughing.

'Yes. I'm Pippo.' Pippo takes an instinctive liking to him.

'Theo,' the smiling man announces, 'and this is my kingdom, for my sins.' He jerks his thumb at the *kafenio* behind him.

'Ah, Theo!' Mitsos has talked about him as if he is an old friend, although he does not look as old as Mitsos. In his mind, anyone over thirty is just old. They all look the same. He can be off by decades; usually is.

'Are you going down to Mitsos's?' Theo asks and rocks from his front foot to his back as if the answer he receives will decide the direction he will next travel.

Pippo looks at Eva, who shrugs.

'Oh well, if you are not, never mind.' Theo doesn't seem concerned.

'No, I can, I mean, I need to see him.' His agreement to help in the shop battles with his desire to spend every second with Eva.

Theo's weight falls on his back foot and with a raised finger, he indicates that they should wait. He skips up the three steps into the *kafenio* and they peer into the gloom after him, watching as he takes a dish from a fridge behind the counter.

'Tell Mitsos it is the lemon peel in at the beginning that makes the difference,' he says, handing the dish over.

Pippo looks at the offering, which has a brown, crusty top.

'What is it?' he asks.

Eva peers at it too. '*Rizogalo*?' she guesses.

'Certainly is.' Theo sounds very proud. 'It is the way my mama used to make it, God rest her soul.' He crosses himself three times and kisses the crucifix around his neck. 'Mitsos used to just lap it up.'

'*Rizi* I know. That is rice, riso,' Pippo says. 'But *rizogalo*?'

'It's a pudding,' Eva explains.

'A pudding with lemon and eggs and cinnamon. This one, if Mitsos still has a taste for it, will probably not last until the anniversary. So if he eats it all, just tell him that Anastasia… I mean *I* will make more.'

Eva laughs. 'You didn't make this at all, did you? Kyria Anastasia made it. How is she, by the way? Please tell her that we do not see enough of her.'

'Ah Eva, you know how she is. Shy as it is possible to be. But maybe she will come to Stella's anniversary.' Theo looks a little sad, as if he does not believe his own words.

'Oh she must come!' Eva presses.

'Is anyone serving here today?' a gruff but jovial voice demands from inside the kafenio. 'A hard-working farmer needs an ouzo!'

'I'd better go.' Theo springs back inside, leaving Pippo and Eva staring into the dish of rice pudding.

'Anastasia won't marry him,' Eva whispers, leaning very close to him. They start to walk across the square. 'They've been together for ages. She's from Athens, and she came here so they could farm olives together, but she won't marry him!' Eva sounds shocked at her own words.

'Any reason?' He waves at Vasso, who is organising empty beer bottles into crates behind the kiosk

Eva shrugs.

'Will you marry?' Pippo says and his heart starts to beat hard.

'I imagine so.'

'I mean me, will you marry me?' Pippo's mouth is instantly dry and he cannot believe he just spoke the words he did. What on earth possessed him? Can he take them back? But does he want to take them back? Instead of looking for his family, he could create a new family!

'Are you serious?' Eva stops walking to look at him. 'We have only known each other a few days. Are you deluded?' She tries to laugh but her focus is fixed. There is sobriety to her question.

Looking at the ground, Pippo searches his deepest feelings and the logic of his mind. Is he crazy?

'I have never felt so sure of anything in my life,' he concludes and looks at her intently. 'So will you?'

A little gasp escapes her lips and there is just a touch of fear, or is it excitement, in her eyes. She is at least thinking about it; she has not said *no* yet.

'If you mean it, Pippo, then you must ask me again in six months' time. Then I will take you seriously.' She speaks with a measured tone.

'Then I will ask you again in six months!' He grins.

'And perhaps you might like to spend those six months courting me! And maybe before you ask me again, we will have kissed.' Now she is teasing him.

'I am serious about this, Eva.'

'I know you are, but I am only just eighteen and your home is in Italy, so a little bit of common sense and logic might be applied here.'

'What I feel for you is not logical.' They resume walking, close enough for their shoulders to touch.

'Nor is what I feel for you, but one of us needs to be a bit sensible.'

'Hey Pippo.' Mitsos interrupts them as they approach the eatery. He is arranging salt and pepper pots on one of the tables out on the pavement.

'Hey, I'm sorry I didn't let you know where I was last night… It was, er, well, a bit awkward.' He feels caught off-guard, not yet sure how much he wants to tell Mitsos. He hasn't even thought about it.

'Nikos set him up and Michalis, the policeman from Saros, caught him,' Eva says.

Mitsos looks up sharply. 'Are you alright, son? What happened?'

Pippo was not sure what he was going to say, but one thing is for sure: he had had no intention of telling Mitsos that much of the truth, and he is a little annoyed that Eva has mentioned it. Being in trouble with the police is nothing to brag about.

'Oh Kyrie Mitso, the whole thing was so unfair and Pippo was such a hero,' Eva says.

Mitsos studies Pippo's face, the trace of a smile on the old man's lips in response to Eva's enthusiasm.

'You know how Nikos and his friends terrorise everyone on their motor bikes,' Eva gushes on. 'Well, basically, they made sure Pippo was taken by Kyrios Michalis rather than them and he had to stay the whole night in Saros police station.' There is awe in her voice.

'That sounds a little harsh,' Mitsos says.

'This is from Theo.' Pippo offers the dish, hoping it will change the subject.

'So you are a jailbird now?' Mitsos takes the dish and winks at him.

'It's *rizogalo*. The way his mama used to make it,' Pippo persists, ignoring the wink.

'Well, you don't look like any harm has come to you,' Mitsos says cheerfully. 'Any chance you could put some charcoal on the fire?'

'I'd better go too; help my mama clear up after the party,' Eva says.

'I'll come…' Pippo says.

'No, you stay and give Mitsos some help, and let me know when you are going to take me for coffee.' She swings her hair over her shoulders and walks away, swaying her hips ever so slightly, as if she is aware that she is being watched. Pippo gazes after her and it is only when she has crossed the square and disappeared from view that he becomes aware that Mitsos is also following her progress.

'Well, I think you have caught her,' Mitsos says and Pippo feels a heat flush up through his cheeks. 'So, tell me your version of what happened with the police.'

Pippo feels it prudent to gloss over the details of his reckless behaviour on the bike, and instead relates an accurate and full account of the night in the police station, which leaves Mitsos laughing so hard, he is red in the face.

'You are not as young and green as you look, are you?' he says, raking the coals with a pair of tongs. 'Well, you've impressed young Eva with your carry-ons. Can you get me six chickens out of the fridge?'

A high-pitched toot toot turns both their heads to the door.

For Mitsos, the days have passed slowly since Stella went to Athens, and it has surprised him to find how used to her company he has become, after spending so many years a single man. The arrival of Cosmo each day gives him a little lift because, bless her heart, she is sending a postcard every single day. She must know how alone he feels without her, or maybe, and it is a selfish but comforting thought, she is missing him so much she is compelled to write.

'Hi Cosmo.' Mitsos shields the sun from his eyes as he steps outside. The postman straddles his bike, engine running, and searches through his sack. It is way too warm for a jacket but Cosmo wears one on all but the very hottest days in August. It is always the same one: grey, with reinforced leather patches on the shoulders, designed to protect against the recoil of a shotgun. Cosmo is not a hunter of course, but the patches stop the strap of his post bag from rubbing.

'No postcard today, but there's this letter. It's on hotel notepaper. It's got their name on the envelope.' Cosmo hands over a pale blue letter. 'I thought she was due back about now?'

'Day after tomorrow, our anniversary.' Mitsos takes the envelope and tears it open with all the eagerness of a schoolboy.

'Oh so that's when you want these dishes?' Cosmo says. 'Maria wonders if she can make biscuits? She has a recipe for savoury ones she says would be a nice appetizer.'

'That would be very kind of her.' Mitsos eyes the letter; his attention is not on Cosmo.

'If she is returning on the day of her party, won't she be tired?' Cosmo asks.

Mitsos unfolds the single sheet. The sight of her handwriting makes him feel less alone. He skim reads and takes a big breath to release tension he did not know he was holding.

'She is coming home tonight!' he exclaims. The happiness he feels is absurd. If he had the balance, he would jump and whoop, but even though he suddenly has all the energy of a teenager, he resists the illusion that he can really perform any such antics and settles for a wide grin.

'Oh, that is good news.' Cosmo slings his satchel over his shoulder and, leaning forward, eases the bike off its stand. 'So, yes to the biscuits then. I will tell Maria, and they are for the day after tomorrow.' He revs his little bike and pootles away up the square no faster than a man could walk, waving to a woman sweeping her steps as he goes and steering wide around a sleeping dog. Finally he turns up one of the side streets and Mitsos goes inside, his head bent over the letter.

'That's great!' Pippo says. 'I cannot wait to meet her.'

'You will love her! She is wild and untamable, and yet caring and domestic. She is so full of positivity I don't think anything could bring her down, not for long, anyway.'

'Has she been in the village all her life?' Pippo asks.

'Ah, yes, you are on a family hunt. I had forgotten.' Mitsos reads over the letter again; it makes him feel closer to Stella. 'Well, she is not originally from here... Well, actually, that's not true. I suppose really she is. He mama is of Gypsy stock, you see, and it was unusual that her mama had a job in the little cheese factory up there by the kafenio. You probably haven't noticed it; all you can see of it from the square is a blank wall. Anyway, her mama worked there and she caught the eye of a man from here and they married and had Stella. So, actually, yes she is from here. I always see her as something more than that, someone bigger than a village girl, funny that!' He could talk about her all day. What a woman!

'Are you making a note of who is bringing what to the party? Do you need to make a note of the postman's biscuits?' Pippo asks as if he has not heard a word Mitsos has said about Stella.

'I suppose I should have done, but I haven't.' The letter does not say what time he should pick her up from Saros. He can hardly go every hour and see if she is on each bus that arrives. 'I'd better just trust her to take a taxi.' He nods and turns the sheet of paper over and then back again.

'What?' Pippo doesn't understand why Mitsos is suddenly talking about taxis.

He lays a third split chicken on the grill. Maybe he should get some chips on.

'Right. I think that fridge needs a clean,' Mitsos says and slings an apron over his head. 'If I do not busy myself doing something, I will spend every minute looking out of the door for Stella,' he explains and kneels in front of the fridge, cloth in hand.

'Ah Mitso.' A breathless voice precedes its owner. Pippo pours chips into the fryer; Mitsos's cloth is abandoned in the fridge. He eases himself up, puffing with the exertion.

'Poppy, how are you? Completely recovered from your accident?' He smiles and holds his hand out to take hers. Pippo likes the way the villagers are so familiar with one another. If two old people stood like that in his hometown, it would be natural to assume they were lovers, but here, standing close, holding someone's hand, or a touch on their arm is so normal. How amazing it would be to spend his life here so that one day, it is he who is standing here like Mitsos, chatting so closely with a neighbour.

'I am very well, thank you. Very well indeed.' She puts her hand on top, so his is now sandwiched between hers.

'Poppy was run over by a bike,' Mitsos explains to Pippo.

'Well, a bike drove very close to me and I fell would be more like the truth!' Poppy laughs. 'And today, now in fact, Thanasis is taking me into Saros.' Mitsos looks over her shoulder, where Thanasis's truck is parked in the square, the passenger door open. 'This will be the first time out of the village since it happened. But Cosmo has just told me Stella is on her way back, so I have just stopped to let you know I am bringing a dish of *dolmades*.' She takes a breath and then adds, 'Only, because I prefer them, I am making them with cabbage leaves, which is what they usually use for the mincemeat *dolmades* with lemon sauce, but I like to break the rules and use cabbage leaves just with rice. Will that be alright?'

'That would be more than alright! Stella is going to love them. If she eats anything at this party, that will be what she will go for,' Mitsos assures her.

'Well, that was it really. Hello Pippo,' she says as if they have been introduced, which Pippo is pretty sure they haven't. It seems he is being absorbed into the village whether he likes it or not!

'Nice woman,' Mitsos comments as she takes her leave. Pippo is aware he called someone else a nice woman—was it Marina? Which means it says more about how Mitsos views the world than it does the women. Mitsos is back on his knees with the fridge door open. The chips are browning and the timer is ticking the countdown. Maybe he needs to think of a dish he can make himself, as a thank you for Mitsos's kindness, and to show his appreciation for the way the people in this village are making him feel like he belongs. And he must take Eva for a coffee. Mitsos will be able to spare him tonight if Stella is back, but then she might be tired. Old people get tired easily. The timer pings and he pours the chips onto kitchen paper laid in the bottom of a deep-sided stainless steel tray, which he then puts on the end of the grill where it is coolest, but still warm.

'She's here!' Mistsos throws the cloth down and pulls himself to his feet as quick as he can. Leaving the chips, Pippo rounds the counter to look out the door. A yellow car is advancing towards them. Mitsos is by his side and the taxi pulls to a smooth stop.

'How did you know she was here?' he asks Mitsos, but the old man is deaf to his voice, his concentration is on smiling at a woman in the back of the taxi who is nothing like Pippo imagined. She is small, almost frail, like a child. Mitsos pulls the door open and the two meet in an embrace, Stella kissing him on any part of his face, neck, and hair she can reach as she stands. She is not tall and, as if to emphasise her petite frame, she is wearing a sleeveless floral print dress that is slightly too big for her. She has dark brown hair that is slightly frizzy, half of which has been pulled into a ponytail at the back; the rest falls to her shoulders.

'Oh my lovely Mitsos, how nice it is to be back!' she says. The taxi driver heaves her case out of the boot and lights a cigarette. Mitsos takes the case inside and Stella pays the driver. They laugh over something Stella says and then she turns, her eyes shining, looking at Mitsos. She marches up to him inside the eatery and with no hesitation, she curves her body against his and kisses him fully on the mouth. Mitsos pulls away, his cheeks burning red.

'Er, darling, this is Pippo,' he says, blinking several times.

Stella's Lemon Roast Potatoes

Stella's lemon sauce recipe is a closely guarded secret, but she recently gave me some tips about how she makes her amazing lemon roast potatoes…

Crispy on the outside, fluffy on the inside with a delicious lemony flavour. Stella's lemon potatoes are perfect on their own served with crusty bread to dig into all the delicious juices or with her roast chicken and a salad!

Selecting the right potato variety for your Greek lemon potatoes is crucial if you want to achieve that perfectly crispy on the outside and fluffy on the inside texture. The ideal type is Maris Piper as they are one of the most starchy kind and will become quite crumbly when baked!

You can parboil the potatoes, i.e. cut them up in wedges, boil them in a pan until right before they are ready and then sift using a colander. Then drizzle with some semolina and the lemon sauce.

Alternatively you can cut your potatoes up in wedges, dress and bake them straight in the oven.

The second approach will take a little longer as the potatoes need to bake for longer but it may give them crispier edges, while the parboiled version allows for more of the lemon sauce to soak in and they tend to be flakier.

The secret ingredient for the crispiest Greek lemon potatoes is in the sauce!

The special sauce is a mix of lemon juice, dried oregano, minced garlic and semolina. Semolina is made from ground up durum wheat and will coat the potatoes and will harden up when cooking, forming a nice crispy skin around them and adding to the crunchiness.

For a large batch of about 7-8 potatoes use 3 garlic cloves, 3/4 of a cup olive oil, equal amount of water (if not parboiled), 1 tsp dried oregano, the juice from 2 lemons and 1 or 2 tsps of semolina, depending on how crispy you like them! Make a little extra just in case the potatoes need a little longer to cook and you have to season again mid-cooking.

Ingredients

7 large potatoes (maris piper)

3 cloves of garlic, minced

150ml olive oil (2/3 cup)

150ml water (2/3 cup)

1 tablespoon dried oregano

Juice of 2 lemons

1 teaspoon semolina

Salt and freshly ground pepper

Directions

Preheat the oven to 200C / 400F / Gas mark 6

Cut the potatoes into wedges and place them on a large metal roasting pan. Into a bowl add the remaining ingredients (including the semolina and the 150ml of water) and blend; pour the semolina-lemon mixture over the potatoes and season well with salt and pepper.

Roast for 40 minutes, until a nice golden crust has formed on the potatoes; turn them out of the oven, toss them a little bit to bring them upside down, sprinkle with a pinch of oregano and put back into the oven for another 30-40 minutes.

If all of the liquid has been absorbed and the pan appears to be getting dry, add 1/4-1/2 of a cup hot water into the pan or some extra lemon mixture, before they have fully browned.

The secret is to sprinkle the potatoes with some semolina, as it helps to form a nice golden crust around them. Don't be afraid of over roasting them- they will become even more delicious!

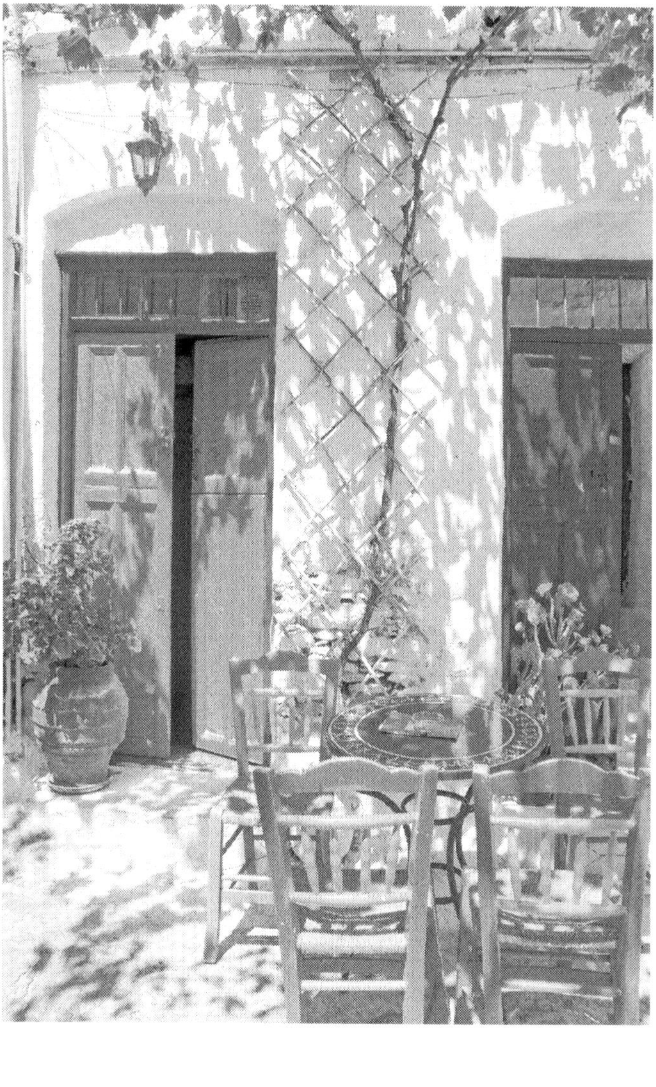

Chapter 13

'It was sort of interesting, but I wouldn't go again.' Stella settles in her chair, obviously tired, but buzzing, excited and full of energy at the same time. 'We were greeted by a team of people in white shirts with clipboards, and shown through to a little anteroom where they gave us name stickers and coffee, but there was nowhere to sit at that point so I went back into the plush corridor and took a chair further down the hall and sat on that. The clipboard people gave me some curious looks.' Two farmers who have come in for chicken and chips call across from the next table.

'What was it you went to?' one asks.

'It was a conference about how to improve the running of your hotel.'

'But you run yours beautifully,' the second farmer says, picking at a chip before Pippo has even put the plate on the table. Pippo stays to listen and looks around the dining room. There is a picture of a sailing boat in a storm on one wall, facing a donkey in a straw hat, flowers in its brim. All sorts of objects have been placed on a narrow shelf high up; a tiny teapot, a plate on its edge, a straw donkey, a horseshoe, an empty bottle of 'mini' ouzo, a china dog, a vase of dried flowers collecting dust.

'Well, I went with an open mind for ways that I could run it better,' Stella says. Mitsos brings her a frappe, with a straw and an umbrella too. She smiles up at him. He sits down beside her and takes her hand. 'Anyway, the speaker was all, "I've done this," and "I've done that," and I wouldn't mind, but he only looked about twelve. He said he had just returned from Las Vegas and that was the sort of lifestyle we should hope to enjoy if we took up his suggestions. As if I would want to go to Las Vegas!' She leans forward to suck on her straw.

'So what did they tell you to do?' Mitsos asks.

'Well, there's the thing. I listened hard and all I heard was what he was "going to tell us," but he never actually got around to telling us any of it. Then he started to say he would expand at the evening seminar and I began to suspect. There was no break, so I snuck out and went and asked about the evening seminar and sure enough, that was one you had to pay for. It was the same on the other days too. And I don't mean just ten Euros or something like that. No, they wanted two hundred euros for the evening seminars. "Free wine," they told me, as if this would make a difference to me!'

'So not free at all!' One of the farmers guffaws.

'No wonder you came back early, dear,' Mitsos says. 'But had you thought that the evening seminar would have been useful, you should have gone.' He says it as if he suspects she did not attend because of the price.

'Well I didn't think it would be useful at all, and nowhere near as pleasant as sitting in my room and writing to you. After that, I went for a wander around Syntagma Square and I watched the evzones marching with their straight legs and their pompom shoes and I had ever such a nice time.' She leans into her husband.

'And the next day?' Mitsos asks.

'The next day was on tax and how to deal with it, ways to pay less of it and how to be "creative." That made me laugh! I mean, the Greeks are past masters at being creative with our taxes.' Everyone in the room laughs, and Pippo joins in although he is not exactly sure what is meant by being *creative with taxes*. Not exactly.

'And did they tell you anything new?' Mitsos asks.

'Oh no, they waffled beautifully for nearly two hours and when I looked at my notes, I realised that yet again, they had not told me anything, really. So at the first mention of the evening seminar, I knew the score. So I left the conference and I went into Plaka and looked at the ruins and had my lunch and went down to that street, I don't know what it is called, the one that just keeps going down. Past Monastiraki until it meets a wide road where they have loads of shops there selling catering equipment. I was in heaven. I found an amazing blender that would be great for making really smooth, creamy fava…'

'So you came back early because it was useless.' One of the two farmers takes his last mouthful and wipes his moustache with a paper napkin from the holder on the table. Pippo realises that he has accepted it as completely normal that these two farmers have joined in the conversation without any invitation. Back in Forte dei Marmi, you could sit in a café all day long and no one from the other tables would make conversation with you.

'I'd better get back to it,' the farmer who has finished says and his friend nods and fills his mouth with the last of his chips and scrapes at the lemon sauce with his knife, which he then licks clean. Mitsos is quickly on his feet and he takes their plates and follows them through to the till.

Stella takes a long sip of her coffee. 'So, Pippo,' she says, 'I am so glad you have been here to help Mitsos. I thank you for that, but tell me, how old are you?'

'Eighteen,' he lies.

'Eighteen, eh?' It is the way she says it. It does not suggest that she does not believe him; it is more of an invitation in her tone, to amend his answer.

'In a few weeks.'

She says nothing.

'In five weeks.' He wants to be honest with her. She seems to encourage this.

'Ah, so it sounds as if what Mitsos has told me is not altogether accurate. It doesn't sound quite like you are taking a gap year.' There is laughter in her voice, as if they are sharing a naughty secret. 'The universities have broken up but school's not out yet, is it?' Her head drops over to one side and she smiles and nods like she understands.

'I couldn't stand it anymore.' For some reason, he whispers this.

'School?' she asks in the same hushed tone.

'Home,' he says even more quietly and he feels the need to suck in his bottom lip, which has started trembling.

'Oh my precious little lamb!' She changes seats so she is closer to him, her arm around his shoulders and despite suddenly feeling protected by her action, his bottom lips quivers all the more and he can feel tears pricking at his eyes. 'Is it your baba?' she asks. He cannot speak so he just shakes his head. She holds him tightly. He thinks Mitsos comes in the room and goes out again just as quickly, but he cannot be sure because he keeps his chin on his chest and for the moment, he cannot look up.

'My mama,' he finally manages to say and her arm around him gives a little squeeze. 'She drinks.' He feels like a traitor. But the secret has been told. For years, at school, with his friends, to himself, he has kept this secret. 'It is not like she is a really big drinker,' he hastens to add. 'But just enough, you know.'

'No, I don't think I do,' Stella says, but he has the impression she actually does.

'It was not like she would fall over and be sick or anything.'

'But…'

'But she would flirt with my friends…' He closes his eyes but of course the images in his head are still there, of his friends treating his mama like she was a tramp, because she was acting like one! 'And my teachers, she would pretend it was a fortuitous accident that she was outside my school when it was home time. She would insist on walking me home. But if she saw a teacher, she would flirt with him as well!' He closes his eyelids more tightly, but it doesn't help. 'And when she was really drunk, late at night, and I know she didn't mean anything by it, but she would talk to me as if I was her partner or something. She would try to get me involved with her plans.' Her drunk voice is in his head right now, cajoling and simpering.

'Plans for the future?' Stella asks, or does she echo, he is not sure.

'Holidays she wanted me to take with her, places we would visit, her dreams that she would never accomplish because she was single and too scared to go alone and I would tell her, "Mama," I would say, and I would be on the verge of saying that I would not go with her anywhere because she was embarrassing, but mostly I didn't want to be with her because she was my mama. I wanted to be with people my own age, you know?'

'Of course you do. That is only natural.'

'But she said it proved I did not love her. She said I would be like all the other men and that I would walk out on her and I kept saying of course I wouldn't.' Pippo is suddenly struck by the reality of his situation. 'But I have, haven't I?'

'I think perhaps you are taking a little break, a small holiday. That's not walking out so much as catching your breath,' Stella says.

'Catching my breath.' It is Pippo's turn to echo. The words bring him comfort and take away the guilt of his being here.

'And Mitsos said you have come here to find your family?'

'That was the original plan.' He turns to look at her, weighs up if he can really trust her. Her face is one of the kindest he has ever seen. 'But I have met someone.' Again he whispers.

'Really?' She does not sound surprised.

'And I am not sure whether what I feel is real or not, but all I know is I want to be with her, like every single minute.'

'Ah.' Stella sounds wise. 'Well, take it from me. If you find a good one, hang on for dear life.' She looks up and Mitsos comes in to join them.

'Well dearest, I am very glad you are home but I am afraid that tomorrow the eatery will be closed,' Mitsos says, slapping his hand down on the table top and then spreading his fingers as if to add authority to his words.

'The eatery is never closed!' She sounds shocked.

'Well, tomorrow it is. For you, anyway.'

'Ah! You are up to something.' She wags a finger at him.

'Yes I am and you know why, and the less you ask, the better.' Mitsos tries to sound authoritative but to Pippo's ears he fails, coming across instead as besotted.

'I see! Plans being made behind my back!' She laughs like a child, with no restraint. 'Well, alright then,' she says as her merriment subsides. 'And I take it you are involved and staying for this mischief that young Mitsos has cooked up?' she asks Pippo.

'I offered him a bed at our house, unless you object,' Mitsos says.

'Of course I have no objection, but I do think a word or two to his mama to say he is just catching his breath would be a good idea.' She stands and Pippo feels a surge of anger towards her, as if she has broken his confidence. She leans over and whispers in his ear. 'She may enjoy a glass too many but, no doubt, she still loves you and will worry.' She says this very quietly and Pippo's rage subsides. Mitsos is frowning, quite obviously not understanding what is going on. 'Now wait a second.' She goes to the windowsill and flicks through the newspapers and magazines stacked there. 'Here you go. A tourist left it.' She hands Pippo a card with a photo of five kittens hanging in socks on a washing line. It is not the type of card he would ever choose, but for some reason, as he looks at it now, it makes him smile, as if the world is a safe place, a world of kittens and stripy socks.

Fava

Fava is sometimes described as a Greek equivalent of Hummus. Simple and tasty!

Ingredients

1 pound / 2.25 cups / 450g dried fava (yellow split peas)

2 whole onions chopped + extra for serving

Salt and Pepper

Olive Oil 60ml

2 lemons

Parsley

Directions

Rinse the fava.

Boil the fava together with the onions and 6-7 cups of water for about 1 ½ hours.

Pass it through a food mill or puree sieve or a food processor.

Put the puree in the pot again and warm up, add some salt, pepper and about ¼ cup of olive oil. Let it come to a boil for a few minutes.

Serve with some chopped (elaborate a little here, such as finely sliced, sprinkled over the top or on the side etc) raw onion, parsley and lemon.

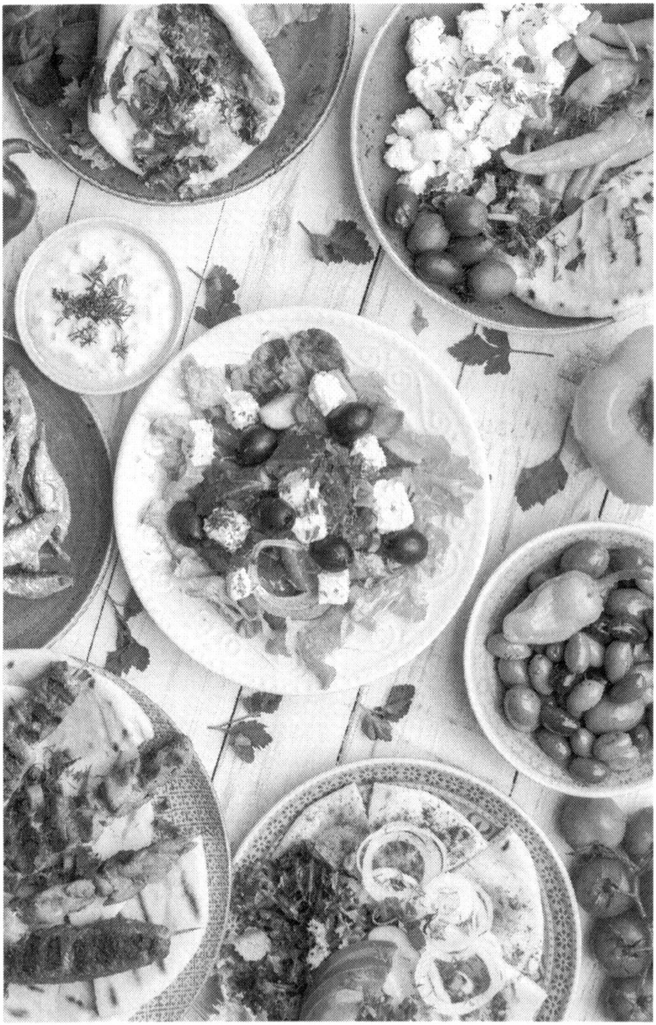

Chapter 14

Sakis strikes up a tune on his guitar that produces a cheer of recognition. Vasso is the first to join in, warbling over the top of Sakis and his guitar and then Theo comes in with a surprisingly deep voice that bellows underneath. Soon the whole village is involved; everyone seems to know the tune and the simple words. The wine has flowed freely over the course of the evening, lubricating parched throats, and as they sing they sway, raising their glasses, heads thrown back.

Stella, at the head of one of the two tables that have been laid out in the yard at the back of their house, is the first to stand and before Pippo understands what is happening, nearly all the villagers are on their feet, arms slung over each other's shoulders, and they create a line that is so long, it circles the two long tables.

Mitsos remains seated, leaning on his crook, and shouts 'Opa!' A couple of the older generation also stay in their chairs but they clap heartily as the villagers snake around the yard. Pippo surveys the table. Everything was so delicious, but if there is any of Eva's baklava left, he will have some.

'Come, come on.' A hand grabs him as the line of dancers passes, and it's too late for the baklava. It is Stella who has invited him to join the dance. He lets her pass; a second hand reaches out to him, beckoning him into the line. It is Athena, Eva's mama, but he remains seated, content to watch for now. Eva is next to her, her eyes glazed over, lost in the music, her feet stepping effortlessly.

Since Stella's return, everything seems to have increased in speed and secrecy. He has been either on some mission or other to help prepare for the party, or involved in sly cover-ups to help Mitsos stop Stella finding out what he is up to. Meanwhile, he has not had a moment to even see Eva, let alone spend time with her. Earlier, she arrived with her family, all of them, and in the meantime, he has felt obliged to stay close to Stella and Mitsos, helping out with anything he could. It is their moment—his can wait, a least a little while.

Athena relinks to the chain, and the line of dancers has moved on. Stella is leading the snaking line of dancers out of the yard and in amongst the walnut trees in the orchard. The moon is full and shafts of light lace their way between the branches. The steps look easy enough to follow; a crossing over of the feet, a shuffle, a step back and then forward again. He can do this. Another drop of wine will help though. He looks around for a bottle. They are all empty, clustered together in the middle of the table. By the cottage are large buckets where beer cans still float in what was ice water. Beer will do just as well as wine. Steadying himself, he makes his uneven way.

'If you're going for beer, I'll have one too.' Mitsos shouts over the music and the singing. The line of people is heading towards him again. Maybe he should leave the beers and join Eva as they pass. He puts the beers back in the bucket and turns to face the dancers. But the song comes to an end, the line of people break up, clapping and laughing.

'Right. Beer for Mitsos,' Stella says, pushing through the crowd before the dancers start again. She gives Pippo a beer too and then, linking arms, walks with him back to their places. 'So,' Stella says, sounding quite drunk. Her eyes are shining, her cheeks are a little red perhaps, but she looks happy in an all-consuming way. He glances around for Eva but he cannot see her.

'So,' Stella repeats, 'I will give the dancing a little break for a moment.' Another tune is already underway and the line of dancers snake around the tables, the footwork little different this time. 'It seems that most of the village is here.' Stella's words are slurred. 'Have you found your family yet? Have you talked to everyone yet? They must be here, right?'

'I have spoken to many of the people here,' Pippo says. He helped arrange the tables and met all the people when they arrived with their dishes of food. Mitsos had taken Stella up past the monastery to look at the sunset over the bay, so the secret would not be revealed till the last minute. 'But I will be honest: I had quite forgotten that I was looking for anyone. I seem to have found so many new friends,' Pippo replies. He could add that it is Eva who most makes him feel like he belongs, but the way he feels about her has become almost sacred and he keeps this to himself.

'So, what do you know about your family here?' Stella says. She takes Mitsos's beer bottle from him and takes a swig, then hands it back. 'Oh, *zeibekiko*!' she exclaims before Pippo has a chance to reply, as a bouzouki starts up. People are starting to dance again, but this time individually, arms spread wide, hips swaying. This might be a good moment to slip away, find Eva, but a hand on his forearm keeps him from leaving. 'Tell me names, places, what you already know.' Stella's attention is back with him.

'Well, not much to tell. I have a cousin, much older than me, who lives back in Forte dei Marmi, and he seems to know the most. He said that his papa would talk, you know, about the good old days, back in… back here. He said most of his family had moved away from here years ago but there was meant to be some lineage left. Well, that was what he said, unless that was just wishful thinking.' He suddenly feels quite drunk; his mind is not focusing properly. He needs to focus. This is why he is here, 'Yes, I remember. The papa would talk of an uncle who was larger than life. Literally, as far as I can make out. Over two meters tall, broad as a horse, a head as large as...' He puts down his beer, opens his hands as if he is holding a large invisible beach ball.

'This, er, giant, was round here?' Stella sounds curious. She picks up his beer this time, takes a swig, and replaces it on the table.

'Yes, from here, and this huge guy would drink whiskey, apparently, a bottle at a time.' Pippo recalls the story.

'No?' Stella's eyes grow wide. His story seems to be captivating her, and he thinks she must be very drunk because he is aware that what he is saying is not that interesting. As he speaks, he is aware of the party continuing around them. A young boy has taken the centre stage and the others have dropped to one knee around him, clapping him on, whistling through their teeth and shouting, 'Opa!' and '*Yeia sou*, Dimitri!'

Stella pats his forearm to bring his concentration back to her.

'Ah yes. This cousin said his baba saw this giant of a man on several occasions perform this sort of party trick with a bottle of whiskey, where he splayed his legs and then bent from the hips, which because of his size was apparently a sight to behold in itself, but then, without putting his hands on the floor, he would pick up the bottle in his teeth and then stand up and tip his head back and drink whatever was left in the bottle.' Pippo had never quite believed this story but it seems an appropriate tale to tell here, in the night, at Mitsos and Stella's wild anniversary party.

'No!' Stella says in response, and Mitsos looks up sharply.

'Yes.' Pippo starts to laugh at the look on Stella's face. She is so comically shocked.

'What was his name?' she demands.

But as he starts to say his name, she speaks too.

'Stantos!' they say in unison.

'How do you know that?' Pippo demands; he suddenly feels cold across his forehead and very sober.

'Stantos the Whiskey Drinker was my mama's mama's second cousin by marriage! Something like that anyway. Everyone in the gypsy community knows, or rather knew, him!'

'Your mama's mama's second cousin,' Pippo repeats and scans her face, taking in what she has said, and just for a moment wondering if she is teasing him. But she looks very serious.

'You know what that means don't you?' Stella's shocked look changes to one of excitement. 'It's me! I am your long lost relative!' And she throws her arms around his neck and she pulls him in for a surprisingly forceful bear hug. 'Mitso!' She lets Pippo go. 'Meet my distant cousin!' She pulls him tight again, and for a moment the party is quiet as his head is trapped between her arms, his nose bent against her bony shoulders, his ears covered.

'I'll drink to that!' Mitsos's muffled voice says and Pippo is released to the chink of Mitsos's beer bottle against his own.

'Marina.' Stella grabs Marina's arm as she passes. 'Meet my distant cousin.' She takes Marina's glass of wine out of her hand and drinks it in one, returning it empty.

'I think you might have inherited some of Stantos's genes,' Pippo jokes with Stella as Marina pats him on the back and mutters something that sounds like 'he belongs anyway.' But she too is slurring her words and she walks away unsteadily, gripping firmly to the backs of chairs as she goes.

Stella takes to her feet as the song Sakis is playing comes to an end. She grabs Pippo's beer bottle and taps it sharply with a knife.

'Everyone, everyone!' she shouts, and a hush falls over the merriment. 'Mitsos and I have been married for three years.' Everyone starts to raises their glasses and mutter congratulations. 'No, wait, there is more. For our anniversary he has given me two of the most amazing things I could wish for...' There is an expectant hush. 'The first is you, every one of you, friends that are more dear to me than I have words to say, and you have all shown me such love and care with your wonderful dishes. This is a day I will remember for some time.' She rubs her stomach as if she is full and pinches at some non-existent fat on her hips to indicate the day will be remembered in more ways than one. There is chuckling and murmurs of agreement. 'The second thing he has given me comes from the mysterious ways of the universe, through him.' There is the silence of suspended animation. 'It turns out that Pippo here,' she puts her arm around him as if she is a proud mama, 'is my distant cousin!' She raises her glass. The noises from the guests are various; some laugh at such joyful news, some mutter, presumably wanting more information, but the majority raise their glasses. Pippo is not sure where Stella is going with her remarks but this party is for her benefit so he quickly picks up a beer bottle; it turns out to be empty but he uses it anyway.

'To Stella and Mitsos,' he toasts and everyone echoes this, and glasses and bottles chink and clash, people shout *'yeia mas,'* and Sakis starts to play a gentle tune.

'I could manage a dance to this,' Mitsos says. Stella, with a kiss on Pippo's cheeks and a promise to talk more later, moves away arm in arm with Mitsos, heading towards the cleared area that is already filling with other dancers. She is very drunk indeed and it is quite a delightful sight to see that it is Mitsos, crook abandoned, who supports her as she gleefully staggers towards the dance floor.

'Hey!' Pippo turns quickly, the voice so close to his ear.

'Hey!' He feels drunk all over again at the sight of Eva.

'You've been busy.' She indicates the tables laid out with all the food.

'I've been waiting,' he says.

'For what?' she asks coyly, as if she has no idea. He slips his hand around her waist and pulls her towards the dance floor.

'For you.' He turns to her and they start to sway in unison.

'And I have been waiting for you.' Her hands fall from his shoulders, her fingers find his, and she leads him gently off the dance floor and under the walnut trees.

'Won't your brothers mind?' He laughs, teasing her, but there a slight seriousness to his question.

'They will have to get used to it.' She makes her way towards the private side of the fattest of the walnut tree trunks, pulling him after her. He follows her willingly, anticipating their first kiss. It must be away from prying eyes, totally in private, or he will lose his nerve. As he pulls her, they spin until her back is against the old gnarled trunk. He pins a hand on either side of her head and moves towards her slowly. She opens her mouth slightly in response. Their faces move towards each other.

'Find your own tree!' The voice startles them, and, peering around the walnut's girth, they find Mitsos pinned against the same tree by Stella. She smiles at the two of them as they walk away.

'She's right,' Pippo says. 'We do need to find our own tree. Our own tree, our own place to live, and our own way of going through life. I asked you before and I will ask you again.' They settle at another walnut tree, this one bathed in a shaft of moonlight. 'Will you please marry me?'

'Ask me again,' Eva says. 'In five months, thirty days, and three hours' time.'

'Not that you are counting!' Pippo says and finally they are nose to nose and their lips find each other's and he is lost in a feeling more magical than he had ever imagined it could be.

If you enjoyed *Greek Island Cooking* please share it with a friend, and check out the other books in the Greek Village Collection!

I'm always delighted to receive email from readers, and I welcome new friends on Facebook.

https://www.facebook.com/authorsaraalexi

saraalexi@me.com

Happy reading,

Sara Alexi

Printed in Great Britain
by Amazon